Charles Seale-Hayne Library

University of Plymouth

(01752) 588 588

LibraryandITenquiries@plymouth.ac.uk

INTRODUCTION TO
THEORETICAL
PSYCHOLOGY

INTRODUCTION TO THEORETICAL PSYCHOLOGY

MICHAEL HYLAND

Department of Psychology,
Plymouth Polytechnic

First published 1981 by
THE MACMILLAN PRESS LTD
London and Basingstoke
Associated companies in Delhi Dublin.
Hong Kong Johannesburg Lagos Melbourne
New York Singapore and Tokyo

Printed in Hong Kong

British Library Cataloguing in Publication Data

Hyland, Michael
  Introduction to theoretical psychology
  1. Psychology
  I Title
  150'.1   BF121

  ISBN 0–333–25826–6
  ISBN 0–333–25827–4 Pbk

Contents

Preface

This is the first textbook to be written solely on theory construction and theory testing in psychology – which is what I term theoretical psychology. In writing it my aim has been predominantly pragmatic: I want psychologists to become more aware of how they should construct better theories, better theories which will then give rise to better and more useful predictions about behaviour. If this book does not lead in the long term to better and more useful predictions then its chief purpose will not have been achieved. There are, however, other advantages to a proper understanding of theoretical psychology. One of them is that it makes it possible to integrate the different areas of psychology. It reveals the theoretical relationship between different sorts of explanation in psychology and shows how empirical research stemming from different areas can be integrated.

There are two things this book is *not*. First, it is not a definitive textbook of theoretical psychology, because theoretical psychology is such an underdeveloped area. It is more of a starting point for further development, and as such it discusses the existing work on the subject as well as including a good deal which is original. Second, it is not a textbook on the philosophy of psychology. It is not written for those who seek a philosophical understanding of mind, matter, man or psychology, nor does it provide such. The only philosophy in the book is philosophy of science, and that is introduced simply to gain a more general perspective of psychological theories.

I have tried to make the book as simple and straightforward as possible. The intention was to make the book comprehensible to final year and postgraduate psychology students taking one of the many courses which have names such as History and Systems in Psychology, Explanation in Psychology and so forth. I hope that this has been achieved. At the same time the book ought to prove useful to all those conducting psychological research and who are seeking a better appreciation of the theoretical basis of their work.

Plymouth 1979   M.H.

1 Why use Theories?

The aim of psychology, like the aim of all other sciences, is to explain things that happen. The particular things that psychologists are most interested in explaining are the thoughts and behaviour of people. Although there is reasonable agreement over *what* psychology should be explaining there is little agreement over *how* these explanations should be effected. One of the characteristics of psychology both past and present is that there is little consensus over *how* thoughts and behaviour should be explained.

An explanation can have a number of characteristics, but one characteristic is common to all explanations: an explanation enables one to predict or postdict the event which is explained. The minimal characteristic of an explanation is that it should enable prediction of the occurrence of the explained event. In any science there are different ways of explaining events, that is, different kinds of or approaches to explanation can be used to predict the same event. Before setting out to explain a particular phenomenon, one therefore has to establish what kind of explanation one is trying to achieve. In the majority of cases, and in particular in the physical sciences, the decision to adopt a particular approach to explanation is carried out automatically because there are well-established ways of explaining physical phenomena. For example, it would be normal to predict whether a bridge stays up or is likely to collapse on the basis of the stresses embodied in the bridge's physical structure. It would be considered decidedly odd if someone predicted that the bridge would stay up because it was consistent with the spiritual growth of man.

Psychology is unusual, if not unique, as a discipline in having very many different approaches to explanation. Psychology also has the characteristic that there are no generally accepted guidelines or conventions about the use of these different approaches. The student of psychology is presented with a bewildering array of physiological explanations, behaviourist explanations, cognitive explanations, phenomenological explanations and psychoanalytic explanations, all of which appear to be very different. And indeed these approaches to explanation do have quite different properties. Perhaps because they appear so different there is hardly any attempt to relate the different kinds of explanation to each other, and those rarely occurring attempts are usually less than satisfactory. At best one learns that there are 'different approaches' to explanation, some of which may be better for explaining one kind of phenomenon and some may be better at explaining other kinds of phenomena. On the whole, however, relationships between approaches are hardly considered and the advocates of one approach not only support their own approach with partisan fervour but also seem to be blissfully ignorant of any other approach. It is a fair comment that modern psychology is broken up into many sub-disciplines with neglible contact between them.

Some psychologists, particularly students who are relatively new to the subject, are dissatisfied with the fragmentation of psychology and seek some form of integration between the different parts. This book tries to help them: it looks at the relationship between different approaches to explanation in psychology and considers current strategies for integrating or relating some of them. The approaches to explanation which are capable of integration will be given the generic term 'theoretical psychology'. Later chapters show how these different approaches fit together into a structure which is both theoretically elegant and able to provide strategies for integrative research in separate areas of psychology.

BEHAVIOURISM *VERSUS* THEORETICAL PSYCHOLOGY

Scientific inquiry leads to a systematisation of information. In any science there are two kinds or two levels of scientific systematisation, the level of empirical generalisation and the level of theory formation (Hempel, 1958). At the level of empirical generalisation, information is systematised by specifying the relationship between observables. Observables are characteristics, attributes or events which can be directly observed. In psychology, the level of empirical generalisation consists of specifying the relationship between stimulus and response, as both stimuli and responses can be directly and publically observed. In a stimulus–response or S–R account of behaviour a set of stimuli are related by some function to a set of responses. Explanation through empirical generalisation would simply require an account of the function relating stimulus to response.

Empirical generalisation

$$Stimulus \longrightarrow Response$$
$$(or\ Independent\ Variable \longrightarrow Dependent\ Variable)$$
$$(or\ Antecedent\ Event \longrightarrow Subsequent\ Event)$$

At the level of theory formation, unobservables are introduced into the explanation. These unobservables, or theoretical terms, are characteristics, attributes or events which are not directly observable, and when used in an explanation they have the property of explaining why particular observables tend to go together. The theoretical description provides a rationale for connections between observables. When psychologists introduce theoretical terms into their explanations they do so by postulating unobservable characteristics of individuals. Naturally, the precise nature of these hypothesised characteristics varies widely between different theoretical approaches, but the hallmark of theoretical explanation in psychology is the incorporation of a theoretical description of the individual. The theoretical description is said to 'intervene' between the stimulus and the response, thus

Theory formation

$$Stimulus \longrightarrow Theoretical\ term \longrightarrow Response$$

Empirical generalisations explain behaviour as the consequence of observable stimuli and observable responses and are sometimes called 'black box' explanations because no attempt is made to look inside the behaving organism. At the level of theory formation explanations in theoretical psychology explain behaviour as the consequence of observable stimuli or situational characteristics, *as well as* unobservable individual or personality characteristics, and hence do attempt to look within the 'black box'. Radical behaviourists (but not neobehaviourists who are considered in chapter 3) advocate explanation by empirical generalisation. According to the radical behaviourist position, no kind of unobservable should be introduced into an explanation; explanations should only be effected in terms of observables. This insistence that explanations should be limited to observables has led to the description *situationism* (Bowers,

1973) as a label for the extreme behaviourist approach to explanation. Situationism means that explanations are given in terms of the situation and not in terms of any individual characteristics which are independent of a description of the situation.

Theoretical psychologists suggest that some form of individual description should be introduced into an explanation. Woodworth (1938) maintains that explanations should take the form S–O–R, where O refers to some organism variable mediating between stimulus and response. Lewin (1938, 1943) suggests that behaviour could be understood as a function of the situational and individual characteristics at a particular point in time. However, the particular form of individual description used varies widely between different psychologists.

Radical behaviourists explain 'how' things happen and so their explanations are sometimes labelled *descriptive*. Theoretical psychology purports to explain 'why' things happen and is therefore sometimes labelled *explanatory*. The labels descriptive and explanatory are a little misleading because an explanation *can* only consist of a description. Theoretical explanations, however, describe events at a level other than the level of events to be explained. It is the property of description at another level which enables theoretical explanations in general and theoretical psychological explanations in particular to explain 'why' observables occur. In the natural sciences, the 'other level' which is used in answering the question 'why' is usually a micro-analysis of the objects being explained. In psychology there are alternative kinds of 'other levels' and this is one reason why theoretical psychology is rather complex.

Whenever a scientist aims to explain a phenomenon he must choose between alternative modes of explanation. At the outset a psychologist has a choice between two alternatives, that of radical behaviourism and that of theoretical psychology. Theoretical concepts are used in theoretical psychology but are not used in radical behaviourism. The decision to choose one or other of these alternatives rests on the *internal* characteristics of each kind of explanation. These characteristics are internal in that they do not depend on the occurrence of external events which the theory predicts. There are many different internal characteristics which have been used to evaluate explanations. For example, one sort of explanation may be considered more useable, or provides a better understanding, or is simpler, or less ambiguous, or whatever internal characteristics are considered desirable in an explanation. It is important to realise that the choice between radical behaviourism and theoretical psychology rests on internal characteristics and not on the *external* characteristic of correct *versus* incorrect predictions. Contrary to some accounts in the literature, the approach to explanation of radical behaviourism or theoretical psychology cannot be 'wrong' in the sense of 'true or false' it can only be 'wrong' in the sense of 'inappropriate'. This is so because the truth or falsity of a statement (or the confirmation or corroboration of a statement) is established by considering the predictions of the statement and seeing to what extent they correspond to observable events. Now it is self-evident that predicted situation–behaviour connections *may* be the same for both levels of systematisation, that is, for radical behaviourist and theoretical psychological explanations. For example (to take a rather extreme case) a radical behaviourist interested in the way early experience affects later behaviour may notice that harsh potty-training leads to a higher probability of keeping one's desk tidy and so he generates an empirical generalisation such as: 'Harsh potty-training in childhood leads to an increase in tidy desk-keeping behaviour in later life', an empirical generalisation which does not include any theoretical term. Alternatively, a psychoanalyst can make the same prediction but this time introduce an explanation involving unobservable happenings within the individual – an account perhaps of anal retentivity. At both levels of explanation, the prediction is the same and so the truth of that particular statement (and only that particular statement) will be the same. When the predictions of two explanations are the same, one cannot differentiate between them on the external characteristic of true *versus* false; the two theories can only be differentiated on the internal characteristic of the appropriateness of the kind of explanation provided. Naturally, a particular theory within one approach may be false, but this does not make the whole approach false. Indeed, any number of theories within an approach may be false, but the most this can suggest is that the approach is, for some reason, not useful – a point which will be returned to shortly. The difference between false *versus* inappropriate explanation is sometimes not appreciated by the (often heated) critics of radical behaviourism who use the possible falsity of Skinner's theory of language development as a basis for concluding that radical behaviourism is false. The particular theory or explanation may be false, but the approach to explanation by means of empirical generalisation cannot be.

As the title implies, this book takes the approach that theoretical psychology provides a better kind of explanation than radical behaviourism on the basis of the internal characteristics of each kind of explanation. Although radical behaviourism is now very much on the decline, such an assertion needs justification and so we will consider some of the arguments for and against these different approaches.

The question of whether to use theories or to use empirical generalisations centres around an argument which has been aptly described by Hempel (1958) as the theoretician's dilemma: the 'Paradox of Theorising' as Hempel called it, is thus

> If the terms and principles of a scientific theory (by which Hempel means theoretical terms) service their purpose, that is, they establish definite connections among observable phenomena, then they can be dispensed with, since any chain of laws and interpretative statements establishing such a connection should then be replaceable by a law which directly links observational antecedents to observational consequences.

The psychological application of Hempel's dilemma is that all theoretical explanations (for example, S–O–R explanations) can be reformulated as S–R explanations, and in so far as the theoretical terms can be eliminated, the question remains, do they in fact add anything to an explanation or are they merely an inconvenience which is better done without? Let us begin by considering the disadvantages of theoretical terms, that is, arguments for the use of empirical generalisations and against the use of theories. The two main arguments against introducing theoretical terms in explanation is their ambiguity, and their tendency to create explanatory fiction. Theoretical concepts in psychology (to a greater extent than in other disciplines) are often poorly described and so add ambiguity to an explanation. Theoretical concepts are often described so loosely that different meanings of the concept can be employed simultaneously. For example, the word 'ego' is used to mean different things by different psychologists. Conversely, one sometimes feels that different authors are meaning the same thing but saying it in different ways. There seems to be some difficulty in communicating the meaning of theoretical concepts and so terms are used inconsistently. However, even if one were certain of the meaning of particular theoretical terms, there would still be difficulties in measuring the theoretical entities they refer to. Something which can only be described theoretically can only be measured indirectly through its behavioural consequences and behaviour may be affected by factors other than the entity which is being assessed. As a consequence, measurement of theoretical entities must always be a hopeful estimate of the entity's value, rather than an absolute certainty. Once theoretical concepts are introduced into an explanation they are difficult to estimate and it may hardly be possible to derive any determinate conclusion from them. Theoretical terms therefore introduce conceptual ambiguity as well as uncertainty in measurement.

A radical behaviourist viewpoint argued by B. F. Skinner is that theoretical concepts should be avoided since they introduce 'explanatory fictions' into an explanation. Suppose that a person laughs a lot and his behaviour is explained by saying that he has a disposition to laugh (or some common language description which is equivalent to a disposition to laugh, such as he is a humourist). Skinner points out that although such an explanation may seem to provide some kind of insight about a person, it actually says nothing more than can be said simply by a description of his behaviour, that is, he laughs a lot. The theoretical concept is merely an explanatory fiction. It is important to realise that part of Skinner's argument is correct. It is certainly true that theoretical concepts are sometimes nothing more than explanatory fictions. However, one cannot conclude from this that all theoretical concepts and all theorising must necessarily be an explanatory fiction. Underwood (1975) suggests that theories should entail at least two theoretical concepts which interact in some way. When a number of theoretical entities interact then theoretical terms are unlikely to be just explanatory fictions as the scope or extent of predictions of the theory is not limited to the prediction (or redescription) of a single behaviour. The more novel and diverse are the predictions made by a theoretical concept the less likely is it to constitute an explanatory fiction.

Theoretical terms do have disadvantages, but they also have their advantages, one being simply that it is sometimes more convenient to be able to employ them. Theoretical terms can be eliminated once, but not before, the relationship between behaviour and prior conditions is known. However, it can be very inconvenient to do without theoretical terms, particularly when ideographic psychology or the psychology of individual differences is being investigated. It will be recalled that in psychology, theoretical terms describe unobservable characteristics of individuals. From a theoretical viewpoint, inter-individual variation is explained by postulating unobservable individual characteristics which differ between individuals and so lead to the prediction of different behaviours between individuals. Radical behaviourism can only explain inter-individual variation in terms of observables occurring prior to the event to be explained, observables which provide a different history for different individuals. Two sorts of historical observables seem to be relevant. First, those observable characteristics occurring during the individual's lifetime which distinguish him from other individuals, and second, those observables which are in some sense relevant to the genetic history of the individual or the individual's ancestors and provide an account of genetic differences. Together these two classes of observables should be able to give a complete account of inter-individual variation, as together they provide an account of the genetic and environmental influences responsible for inter-individual variation. Theoretical psychologists can (but need not) give an ahistorical account of inter-individual variation; radical behaviourists *must* give an historical account.

In practice, the kind of elimination of theoretical terms described above is often rather inconvenient. It is really rather difficult to establish precisely what has happened to an individual when he was young and it is even more difficult to give an account of observables which occurred during some remote genetic history. And even if such information were available, it is considerably more unwieldy than a theoretical description. The point is that it is only reasonable to give an account of individual variation in terms of observables when the observables responsible for the individual variation are relatively recent. If one is interested in individual differences in rats – for example, in individual differences in amount of eating behaviour – then an account of rat variation in terms of hours of food deprivation can certainly replace an account of rat variation in terms of some internal drive state. However, in some cases of human variation, theoretical elimination is in practice almost impossible as the individual variation is the consequence of much more distant events. For example, it would be extremely difficult to explain complex verbal behaviour, and hence thoughts, on the basis of previous environmental and genetic influences, even though it should be possible in principle – as presumably the individual and hence his thoughts are the consequence of environmental and genetic influences, rather than, say, supernatural influences. Thus, the behaviourist argument that explanations can just as easily be effected without theoretical terms is not always true. There are certainly phenomena which are much more easily or more conveniently explained through the use of theoretical concepts.

It must be re-emphasised that the argument for incorporating theoretical terms into explanations is one of convenience rather than necessity, as it must be possible to give some form of observable representation to any theoretical concept (see Maxwell, 1962). Contrary to the assertions of crusading phenomenologists it *is* possible to explain behaviour without taking an individual's thoughts into account. However, the avoidance of theoretical concepts may mean a commitment to the impossible task of tracking down observables in the forgotten past.

Theories have one important advantage over empirical generalisations: the additional information embodied in a theory, information about *why* relations between observables occur, provides a more comprehensive set of predictions which is extremely valuable while knowledge is still being acquired. Although theoretical terms may, in principle, be replaceable by statements about observables, they are often considered indispensable during the acquisition of knowledge (Maxwell, 1962).

An empirical generalisation provides a system of prediction which is limited to the observables described in that particular explanation. If an empirical generalisation informs us that observable O_1 leads to behaviour B_1 then this gives no information about the kind of behaviour observable O_2 is likely to produce. Empirical generalisations are generalisations about a particular set of observables and it is not possible to generalise from these observables to others.

In a theoretical explanation, on the other hand, the use of a theoretical concept can enable predictions of events which are quite different from those under which the theoretical concept was initially inferred. As long as the theoretical concept is relevant it can be used for predictions in novel situations. Unlike empirical generalisation, theoretical explanations enable generalisation beyond the results of a particular observation or type of observation.

The ability to generalise beyond a set of observations has tremendous practical significance. Many psychologists feel that their science should have some practical value. For example, psychology should provide a procedure, or at least give advice, as to how certain undesirable psychological or social problems may be best changed. One difficulty with ascertaining how to change a particular set of observables is that experimentation on human subjects may be limited for purely ethical reasons. It is not possible to submit humans to the stresses which can be applied to physical materials. One cannot, like engineers, stress materials to their destruction. The disadvantage of using empirical generalisations as an explanation for a phenomenon is that they provide no knowledge about how to change the phenomenon, because changing a phenomenon is a different observable from the phenomenon itself. Authors concerned with the applicability of research findings have long been aware of this limitation of empirical generalisations (for example, Williams, 1947; Mack and Snyder, 1957; Tizard, 1976). If knowledge of a particular phenomenon is based on empirical generalisations, then, if one wishes but does not know how to change that phenomenon, all that is possible is to manipulate variables until the right combination turns up. Such a 'sock it and see' approach, however, may not be feasible when dealing with humans. It is not possible to find out how to overcome the effects of maternal deprivation by depriving some children of their mothers and then manipulating their environment in some way; schizophrenia cannot be cured by comparing a control group with experimental groups entailing randomly modified en-vironments. The advantage of the theoretical approach to expla-nation is that the theory provides some account of why a particular phenomenon occurs and so gives at least a hunch as to the kind of variables which are likely to be effective in changing that pheno-menon (Tizard, 1976). The additional information present in a theoretical explanation can provide invaluable guidance when trying to apply an understanding of people gained in the laboratory and elsewhere to problems in the outside world.

The great advantage of theoretical explanations in psychology is that they provide a more *useable* explanation of phenomena, that is, they provide an explanation which can be more readily applied. An interest in theoretical psychology is not an ivory tower pursuit with no bearing on the real world. Good theories provide that more complete understanding of phenomena which is necessary to predict what strategies are likely to be effective. If psychology is to be a useful science, data are not enough; theories are needed as well.

DATA, THEORIES AND THE HISTORY OF SCIENCE

Explanations at the level of theory formation provide an account of *why* connections between observables occur. At the same time, a theory often goes beyond its initial predictions to predict associations amongst observables which have not been investigated before. Historians of science have stressed the importance of theoretical formulation as a mechanism for guiding and generating empirical research. By analysing the way successful sciences have developed in the past, historians of science have noticed the importance of theoretical development in the growth of a science. There are two influential accounts of the history of science which we shall apply to the existing state of psychology, those of Kuhn and of Lakatos.

Kuhn's (1962) analysis of the history of science introduces two key concepts, the concept of a paradigm and the concept of normal science. A paradigm consists of a generally accepted system of ideas which defines the legitimate problems and methods of a research field. Once a paradigm has come into being then research workers working within the confines of the paradigm engage in normal science. Following overall guidelines, they 'mop up' specific anomalies and problems. Kuhn shows how paradigms sometimes change by a process of 'scientific revolution' but he also suggests that some sciences have not yet achieved their first paradigm. All sciences initially go through a *preparadigmatic stage* when there is no common agreement about the methods or direction of the science. The nature of preparadigmatic science can be illustrated by its disadvantages.

In the absence of a paradigm or some candidate for paradigm, all of the facts that could possibly pertain to the development of a given science are likely to seem equally relevant. As a result, early fact-gathering is a far more nearly random activity than the one that subsequent scientific development makes familiar. Furthermore, in the absence of a reason for seeking some particular form of more recondite information, early fact-gathering is usually restricted to the wealth of data that lies readily to hand . . . But although this sort of fact-collecting has been essential to the origin of many significant sciences, anyone who examines, for example, Pliny's encyclopedic writings or the

Baconian natural histories of the seventeenth century will discover that it produces a morass. (p. 16)

Much of the empirical research carried out in psychology seems to have the arbitrary directedness characteristic of preparadigmatic science. Later Kuhn says – in a way that would aptly describe psychology today: 'No wonder, then that in the early stage of the development of any science different men confronting the same range of phenomena, but not usually all the same particular phenomena, describe and interpret them in different ways.' (p. 17)

Psychology does not have the coherence and general agreement that is the characteristic of a normal science. It is true that there is substantial agreement *within* one of the approaches to psychological explanation, but there is certainly little agreement *between* the various approaches – physiological, cognitive, social, phenomeno-logical and psychoanalytic to name but a few. More often than not a paradigm emerges from the preparadigmatic state because one particular approach is more successful than the others. Perhaps the emergence of one particular approach is not the way that psychology will develop. The view of this book is that the different approaches should be integrated within a general theoretical structure. Integration, however, is a popular and often meaningless word. Integration does not mean that social psychologists will sometimes talk to physiological psychologists. The integration must have practical consequences; an overall explanatory structure should emerge in which approaches to explanation fit together to form a more comprehensive kind of explanation. The later chapters of this book are based on this assumption.

Lakatos's (1971) analysis of the history of science differs in some respects from that of Kuhn, but the same kind of conclusions about psychology can be drawn. Lakatos's unit of analysis is that of the *research programme*. A research programme consists of a 'con-veniently accepted *hard core* with a *positive heuristic* which defines problems, outlines the construction of a belt of auxiliary hypotheses, forsees anomalies and turns them victoriously into examples, all according to a preconceived plan'. Lakatos makes the further point that 'it is primarily the positive heuristic of his programme, not the anomalies, which dictate his choice of problems'. Lakatos suggests that research programmes can be evaluated in terms of advancing and degenerating problem shifts. Advancing problem shifts occur when theory precedes data, that is, it is the theoretical ideas which govern the empirical research. Degenerating problem shifts occur when empirical research precedes theory; theories are proposed after the acquisition of data. Lakatos suggests that advancing problem shifts characterise the more successful advances of a science. Theoretical speculation provides a systematising impetus to the development of a science.

On the whole, psychological research seems to follow the pattern of a degenerating problem shift. Psychological research is primarily data or methodology orientated: theories play a relatively small role (relative to, say, physics). Psychology, more than any other discipline has been influenced by logical positivism, a doctrine which specifically rejects the introduction of speculative theoretical concepts. Long after logical positivism was rejected by physicists and later by philosophers of science, psychologists have still been loyally following their restrictive charter. In their attempt to be scientific, psychologists have been following a scientific method which no one else these days believes in. Psychologists have been collecting facts, not theories. However, research habits are difficult to break: psychologists are trained to use their hands and not their heads; they are trained to collect facts accurately and without bias, not to think about what to do with them. On the whole, they are collected for their own sake, not because they confirm or falsify a theory. There is certainly more than a grain of truth to the typical student complaint that academic psychologists collect facts without considering whether they will have any use.

One answer to the current dissatisfaction with psychology is that scientific psychology is an unattainable aim and that one should instead try some new, radical, non-scientific approach. An alternative argument is that scientific psychology has not yet been given a chance. Scientific psychology or psychology as a natural science must entail a theoretical psychology and theoretical psychology is still very much in its infancy.

In the psychological literature, books sometimes appear which, like this one, suggest a new road for psychology. Colleagues sometimes tell me that they start these books with a feeling of hope which gradually diminishes as the end is reached, when they realise that nothing particularly new or useable has come out of it. If the reader has experienced this kind of disappointment, a little anticipated reinforcement can be given before the subsequent chapters are tackled: first, this book will show how to construct clear and logically consistent theories; second, it will consider how psychological approaches can be integrated and make suggestions for integrative research.

2 Introduction to Theories: Predictive Power, Form, Content

The purpose of this chapter is to introduce some of the concepts or characteristics which are used in the construction of theories. Almost all of these concepts will be considered in greater depth in later chapters, but it is useful to begin with a framework or common language in which to place them.

What are the characteristics of a 'good' theory? The most important characteristic of a good theory is that it can be tested and when tested it should receive empirical support. A theory should be true in the sense that observable facts correspond to the predictions of the theory. This characteristic is *the* basic criterion for evaluating a theory and is often referred to as an external criterion. It is an external criterion in that it involves a consideration of things which are external to the theory, that is, events which occur in the outside world. How theories are tested, how it is established whether they are true or false is considered in the final chapter of this book.

In addition to the external criterion, theories can also be evaluated in terms of a number of internal criteria. These internal criteria reflect what are considered to be desirable characteristics of a theory and so there are slight variations in the particular criteria recommended. They are internal criteria because they can be applied to a theory without having to take into account any characteristics which are external to the theory, such as events which happen in the outside world. Amongst the internal criteria most often cited are those of parsimony, internal consistency, responsiveness to new data, and stimulation value.

If two theories explain the same set of data then the theory which appears the simpler or more parsimonious is considered to be the better theory. A theory should not be too complex or it loses the

parsimony – extreme care of reluctance of spendin

advantage of simplification which is one of the arguments for the theoretical reformulation of data in the first place. This is not to say that theories should always be simple: complex data may call for complex theories. However, a theory which can explain a particular set of data *more* simply is considered to be better than one explaining the same data in a more complex manner. The terms of a theory should be internally consistent or the theory will be confusing or ambiguous. A theory should, after all, be logically possible. A theory should be sufficiently flexible to incorporate new information if and when it is discovered, and a theory should stimulate further empirical research. Each of those internal criteria (which are not necessarily independent) can be emphasised and elaborated to a greater or less extent. However, there is one internal criterion which is often not mentioned and yet seems to embody those characteristics which would in the first instance induce one to adopt a theoretical approach to explanation. This criterion also encapsulates some of the meaning of the other criteria just cited and for these reasons it will be presented as *the* most important internal criterion: the criterion is that of predictive power.

Predictive Power

Psychological theories contain two kinds of information, existential information and predictive information. Existential information provides knowledge about the nature of people, what they consist of, how they function, what the parts are and so on. Predictive information provides knowledge about things that happen, what people are likely to do or say. The amount of predictive information embodied in a theory is commonly called empirical content, or predictive power (Popper, 1963). It is usual to define empirical content in terms of the observables a theory predicts will *not* occur. Popper makes the point 'a theory tells us the more about observable facts the more such facts it forbids'. The empirical content of a theory is high when there are many potential falsifiers of a theory (that is, potential observations which contradict the theory); the empirical content is low when there are relatively few potential falsifiers. The statement 'It will only rain on Tuesday next week' is potentially more falsifiable and provides a better prediction of events than the statement 'It will rain next week'. Thus a theory which provides good predictive information is one which makes 'bold conjectures', conjectures which are potentially easily falsifiable.

Psychological theories are often constructed in such a way that they are extremely difficult to falsify. Some psychoanalytic theories, for example, are almost completely unfalsifiable. The motivation to construct these difficult-to-falsify theories may stem from the fact that they stand up rather well against critics who wish to show them wrong. However, low empirical content is a serious drawback when one looks to the theory to make predictions. Popper makes the point that 'a hypothesis may be very probable simply because it tells us nothing, or very little'.

Existential information is useful in that it tells one about the nature of people and hence provides a framework justifying the application of particular procedures. For example, psychoanalytic theory which is high in existential information but low in empirical content provides a rationale for the use of psychoanalytic techniques even though it provides very poor predictions about what a person is likely to do or say. The presence of existential information is an advantage. Psychoanalytic theory allows one to make sense of bizarre or unusual behaviour, it provides a framework for conceptualising the antecedents to behaviour which would otherwise seem inexplicable. On the basis of psychoanalytic theory one employs a particular kind of methodology for gaining insight into a person's mind and one uses a particular kind of therapeutic technique to overcome psychological disturbances. However, psychoanalytic theory does not provide precise predictions about what is likely to happen. Psychoanalytic theory may provide an explanation *after* the event has happened but it tells one very little about what will happen given that a particular set of conditions have occurred. Harsh potty-training does not necessarily lead to keeping a tidy desk nor can the success of a therapy procedure be predicted with any degree of accuracy. Theories which are high in predictive information have the advantage, if true, that they enable one to anticipate events. Because one knows what is likely to happen it is possible to arrange external conditions in such a way that desired outcomes are attained. Existential information provides a kind of understanding of behaviour but predictive information enables accurate control of behaviour. The knowledge of what is likely to happen is essential if remedial programmes of change are to be attempted, and so theories must be high in predictive information if psychology is to be a useful and practical science. Theories must not only reveal what man is like, they must also predict what man will do.

One objective of theoretical psychology must be to improve the predictive power or empirical content of theories. Psychological theories should make precise useable predictions rather than general, unspecific, unuseable predictions. In other words, psychologists should try to construct highly falsifiable theories, but theories which upon testing are *not* shown to be false. The formulation of precise highly falsifiable predictions does not necessarily mean that those predictions should be deterministic, though, naturally, deterministic theories will tend to have better predictive power than those involving a lot of uncertainty. However, if non-deterministic or statistical theories are proposed, then an objective characterisation of the uncertainties involved in the predictions should be sought. Although it may not be known for certain whether an event will occur, one should be able to specify the likelihood of its occurrence as in doing so one provides a more falsifiable theory and hence a theory with better predictive power. Although psychology may sometimes (perhaps the majority of cases) be able to produce only a statistical prediction, nevertheless this statistical prediction can still be formulated precisely, as in doing so the degree of uncertainty of prediction is reduced.

Prediction on a statistical basis may occur for one (or a combination) of two reasons: either because the processes themselves are intrinsically statistical, or because certain 'hidden variables' influence a deterministic process in such a way that only statistical interpretation is possible. Whether or not processes are intrinsically statistical it seems self-evident that uncertainty in psychology is contributed to by hidden variables, that is, variables whose existence or characteristics are unknown. The less hidden variables there are, the smaller will be the uncertainty or tolerance limits within which events are likely to occur, and the higher will be the empirical content of the prediction.

DESCRIBING A THEORY

The words which are used to describe a theory are of two kinds. Some of the words are names or characteristics of individual things (for example, aggression, reinforcer, rate of response, happiness). These descriptive or non-logical terms describe what is conventionally called the *content* of a theory (Brodbeck, 1968). Other words are used when the words making up the content are put together into sentences. These other words specify connections between the content (for example, 'leads to', 'of . . . then', 'or', 'and') and are usually referred to as the *form* of the theory. The content comprises non-logical terms whereas the form comprises logical terms. (Incidentally, the distinction between form and content is a general one which is not just restricted to theories. In music, for example, form would consist of the relationship or order of notes, whereas content consists of the values of the notes themselves). To illustrate the difference between form and content of theories, consider the two sentences: 'Frustration leads to aggression' and 'Frustration sometimes leads to aggression'. These sentences have the same content but have differing form. However, the sentences 'Frustration leads to aggression' and 'Frustration leads to anxiety' have differing contents but have the same form.

Psychologists are sometimes criticised for describing their theories in ways which are ambiguous, and in particular for using the same term to mean different concepts. Ambiguity must be avoided because it prevents accurate communication of ideas and hence prevents the integration of related research. Ambiguity can also reduce the empirical content of a theory. Ambiguous characterisation of a theory can result either from an ambiguous description of the content of a theory or an ambiguous description of a theory's form – or both.

Form

How can we make sure that the form of a theory is being expressed accurately and precisely? As the form can be expressed through common language terms, one course of action is simply to make sure that the sentences of a theory are written as clearly and un-ambiguously as possible. When using the logical terms of language, care should be taken to ensure that theories are written in such a way that only one interpretation of the logical terms is possible. However, the logical terms of common language are not absolutely precise and ambiguity in the description of the form of a theory can be reduced still further by using a system of logical expressions which is more precise than the logical terms of common language. The course usually adopted is to describe the connections between the content of a theory by using the logic of mathematics. The content of a theory is represented by symbols and the form represented by a mathematical expression which specifies relations between these symbols. The mathematical expression provides a precise characterisation of relationships. When a theory is expressed mathematically, the logic of mathematics is employed to describe the logical terms of the theory, and the theory takes the form of a mathematical expression in which various symbols in the expression refer to parameters defined in the content of the theory. (Note that only the form but not the content is defined mathematically.)

What are the main features of mathematical expression of psychological theories? The most useful mathematical expression to the psychologist is the equation. An equation specifies equivalence between the elements of two sets, that is, the function specified in the equation pairs up an element in one set with an element in another. Psychologists use an equation's ability to pair up elements for prediction: the parameters on one side of the equation usually represent antecedent events and on the other side subsequent events:

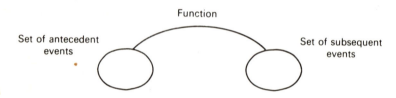

Function

Set of antecedent events

Set of subsequent events

Prediction in time, that is where there is a time difference between equivalent elements in either set, is the most common use of equations but equations can also be used for prediction between simultaneously occurring events. By using an equation it is possible to give a mathematical expression to the terms 'if . . . then' or 'if . . . sometimes'. Most important, the word 'sometimes' can be given a precise probabilistic rendering which is very useful for precise description of uncertainties. The use of mathematical expression is that it provides a precise characterisation of the logical terms in a theory.

Mathematics, or at least quantitative mathematics, expresses parameters on a ratio scale; when a psychological theory is expressed mathematically, the content of the theory should also be represented on a ratio scale. To put it another way, one must have sufficient information about the values of the parameters in a psychological theory to make it worthwhile expressing the theory mathematically. Evidently, precise prediction from unmeasurable or vague parameters is not possible. However, given that parameters can be estimated with reasonable accuracy on a ratio scale, then the mathematical expression will give a precise rendering of *combinations of different* parameters. For example, when two parameters are known to combine, the combination can be expressed mathematically, either as an additive function, or as a multiplicative function, or as a combination involving different weights, or whatever seems appropriate. Thus, the mathematical expression not only provides a precise rendering of logical terms but it does so in terms of a precisely characterised account of combinations amongst the different parameters which form part of the content of a theory.

In the case of quantitative mathematics, there is always an assumption that parameters are measureable on a ratio scale. Recently, there has been an attempt to use qualitative mathematics to specify the form of a theory as qualitative mathematics avoids the requirement of a ratio scale. Catastrophe theory (Zeeman, 1977), a branch of qualitative mathematics, has been applied in a number of disciplines, including psychology. One advantage of catastrophe theory is that it can describe the form of a theory where continuous change along one parameter results in discontinuous change along some other parameter. Some behaviours seem to have an element of discontinuity and the processes underlying such behaviours may (but need not) entail a form such as those described in catastrophe theory.

Mathematical psychology, that is the mathematical specification of the logical terms in a psychological theory, first became prominent in the nineteen-fifties, and since that time a limited number of psychological theories have been expressed mathematically. Given the potential improvement in precision from the mathematical expression of a theory, it is perhaps surprising that mathematical psychology has not been more successful or widespread. One possible reason is that mathematics has, on the whole, been applied to rather simple behaviouristic theories which are themselves not very informative. However well the form of a theory is described, good characterisation of the form will never make up for a poorly described or inadequate content. A theory with form but little content is unlikely to lead to useful predictions. In that mathematics has only been applied to simple theories about simple (and possibly trivial) behaviours, it is not really surprising that mathematical psychology has not made a greater impact on psychological theories.

Indeed, mathematical psychology seems to have been most successful in the more complex theories where there has been theoretical content, for example, the theoretical concept of utility used in decision theory.

There is sometimes amongst students a prejudice that mathematical psychology is 'wrong', on the mistaken assumption that it seems to reduce people to numbers or some other misunderstanding of the nature and purpose of mathematical psychology. These conceptual prejudices must be avoided. All that mathematics can do is to give a precise rendering of the logical terms in a theory, terms which are normally expressed less precisely in common language; mathematical psychology can do no more than this. As yet it is not known whether it is more useful to represent the form of psychological theories by common language logical terms; whether it is better to use the logic of mathematics; or whether it is better to use some other form of logical description. Mathematical formulations certainly seem to be necessary when the form of a theory is complex and, in particular, where there are complex combinations of parameters to be expressed. However, not all psychological theories will involve such complexities and in simpler cases common language expressions may be more appropriate.

Models

Isomorphism is the property of the logical terms of a theory: when two theories have identical forms, they are said to be isomorphic. Isomorphism is a useful property from the point of view of constructing a theory because it enables a new theory to be *modelled* on an old. If the form of an established theory is adopted as the form for a new theory, then the established theory is acting as a *model* for the new. The term model is used for isomorphic theories where the form of the new theory or 'model' is isomorphic with that of the established theory.

Suppose one wishes to construct a theory about a set of parameters, and these parameters seem to behave in a similar way to some other parameters about which there is an already established theory. In such a case it is reasonable to presume that the new theory *may* be isomorphic with the established theory and so a new theory can be constructed using the logical terms of the established theory as a basis for constructing the new theory. In doing so the terms comprising the content of the established theory are replaced on a one-to-one basis by new terms which constitute the content of the new theory. For example, there is an established theory about the spread of disease, and rumours seem to spread like diseases, so a theory of the spread of rumour can be constructed using the form of the theory of the spread of disease. The content of the theory of disease is replaced by a new content referring to the characteristics of rumour: the term physical contagion is replaced by verbal contagion, barriers to infection substituted for by some social equivalent such as resistance to belief, and so on. It should be noted that when a new theory is modelled on an established theory, the established theory gives no guidance as to the nature of the new content; it simply indicates when it is needed and specifies the relations between the different terms.

Mathematical models occur when a mathematical theory is used as a model for an empirical theory. Mathematical theories have no content, they contain no empirical statement. (An empirical statement is one which can be shown to be true or false on the basis of observation. Mathematical theories consist of tautologies and are not shown true or false on the basis of observation. The truth of mathematical theory is that of tautological truth.) When a psychological theory is modelled on a mathematical theory, one simply attaches content (that is, empirical meaning) to the mathematical symbols. When mathematical theories are used as a model for psychological theories, content is not replaced, content is simply attached.

The use of models is just a heuristic for constructing theories. When one uses a model one simply borrows the form for a new theory from somewhere else: models are nothing more than that. For example, the truth of the theory which is used as a model has no bearing on the truth of the theory which is modelled on it. Models are theories like any other and must be tested accordingly.

A model is an isomorphic theory; however, the term model is also used by psychologists to mean other things. Using one word to mean different things is a recipe for confusion and so other meanings of the word model should be avoided. A model is not an untested or untestable theory; it is not a little theory; it is not a theory which one feels guilty about; it is not a theory which is badly formulated – if a theory corresponds to these descriptions one should say so, not call it a model. Psychologists also use the term model to refer to theoretical terms. This practice is not entirely incorrect because the relations between the theoretical terms may be the same (isomorphic) as relations amongst other objects on which the theoretical terms are modelled. However, the term model does not signify that a concept is theoretical, rather it signifies that the theoretical concept or concepts are isomorphic with some other concepts. In that there are adequate labels for 'theoretical terms' ('hypothetical construct' and 'intervening variable') it would be less confusing if the term model was not used for theoretical concepts of any description.

Content

So far the focus has been on the logical terms or the form of a theory. The description of a theory's form, however, does not present too much of a problem. After all one can always draw on the examples of other disciplines to see how their logical terms are described. Indeed one can if one so wishes use the form of a theory in some other discipline as a model for a theory in psychology. It is not the description or the formulation of the form of a theory which introduces peculiar problems for psychology, as these problems occur in all disciplines. Rather, it is the description and formulation of the non-logical terms or content which constitute the theoretical challenge for psychologists. The psychologist is faced with a problem as to what terms or what kinds of terms should be admitted into the content of psychological theory. This book is primarily concerned with examining the content rather than the form of psychological theories. Information is currently available which describes theories entailing highly sophisticated and precise forms. However, there is little guidance on how to select and describe the content of a theory.

Theoretical psychology was defined in chapter 1 as explanations of behaviour which incorporate both an account of the situation and of the individual. The content of explanations in theoretical psychology therefore comprises three different sorts of concept; behaviour, the situation and the individual. Both behaviour and the situation are observables: they can be observed. Individual characteristics, however, are theoretical concepts: they cannot be observed. The individual characteristics will be examined in the next chapter since they introduce a number of problems.

The distinction that has been made between observable and theoretical terms is actually one of convenience. It is generally accepted that it is not possible to classify terms on a dichotomy of observable *versus* theoretical; rather terms fall on an observable/

theoretical continuum. (For example, a bacteria viewed under a microscope is less observable than a fly viewed through glasses, which in turn is less observable than an apple seen with the naked eye.) The observable/theoretical dichotomy is used because for most purposes it is a simpler and perfectly adequate characterisation of terms.

All observables (and that includes observables in physics) are to some extent *theory laden*, that is, they all involve some theoretical interpretation. To put it tritely, all terms are theoretical, but some are more theoretical than others. When describing any observable, whether it is a situation or a behaviour, the description entails an interpretation of what is seen. Sometimes one is aware of different possible interpretations, as in the case of reversing figures, but often only one is considered. If someone were to approach another with raised fists, a snarl on their lips and shouting obscenities, most people would call the behaviour threatening. However, it may be said that the behaviour was part of a fertility dance, or a warning of impending danger, or a sudden muscular spasm, or something else, and that the behaviour was not threatening. Thus, the description of an observable event may be wrong because in order to describe it, what has been seen must first be interpreted. Any description is based on an interpretation of what is seen and therefore involves some element of subjectivity. The existence of subjectivity means that one is never absolutely certain that events are truly as described. It is probably true to say that the observables with which psychologists concern themselves tend to be more theory laden than observables in other disciplines, but it is a difference of degree rather than of kind. Although physicists tend to ignore (quite justifiably) the theory ladenness of many of their observables, that is not to say that those observables are without an interpretative element. It needs emphasising that theory ladenness of psychological observables is not unique and is not something which should necessarily lead to a rejection of the scientific approach to an understanding of man – though it may induce particular caution when describing observables. Some people have argued along the lines that people can never be understood scientifically, because one can never get 'outside' a person to observe objectively; however, the same comment could be applied to any other science. True objectivity is never attained; one *can* never get 'outside' to make sure that the description involves a correct interpretation of events, but that does not prevent the successful carrying out of scientific endeavours. The theory ladenness of observables in psychology may sometimes be a problem, but it is not *a priori* an unsurmountable barrier to the scientific study of man.

When there is consensus in the description of a behaviour or situation then it seems unnecessary to direct much attention to the act of interpreting or the theory ladenness of the observables, though one must always recognise the possibility that an interpretation may be incorrect. Although true objectivity does not exist it is conventional practice (both in psychology and in other sciences) to assume objectivity where one is reasonably certain of the interpretation of an observable. If there are errors in interpretation, then these errors will soon manifest themselves by the falsity of the theories using the erroneously conceived events. The assumption of objectivity helps the construction of theories as it gives one a starting point to work from, and after all, it is an assumption unlikely to lead to undetectable errors.

When differences in the interpretation of observables do occur, then these differences are the result of different characteristics of the interpreting individuals. When differences in interpretation occur, the researcher cannot ignore his own individual characteristics, but should try to establish what characteristics about himself lead him to interpret the situation or behaviour in the way he does and then make his conclusions explicit to others. By making his assumptions explicit he will avoid misunderstandings with other researchers who may possibly interpret the behaviour or situation in a different way. One must not over-react to the theory ladenness of observables. The only recommendation that seems necessary is for researchers to check their interpretation of events against the interpretation of others (which involves asking people what they think) and if there is consensus then one can feel more confident in the correctness of the interpretation.

Behaviour

Theoretical psychology is concerned with explanations of behaviour. Behaviour can be classified so as to distinguish different kinds or different sorts of behaviour, and one way of doing so is to use the way behaviour is measured as a distinguishing criterion. There are three different ways of measuring behaviour: the measurement of overt movements; the measurement of verbal statements; the measurement of physiological responses. These different sorts of behavioural measurement give rise to three different ways of describing the data to be explained. They provide different sorts of psychological data. A psychologist may be interested in explaining overt movements; he may be interested in explaining experiences as manifested in a subject's verbal reports; or he may be interested in explaining physiological responses made by the subject. In later chapters it will be seen that the way behaviour is measured has important consequences for theory construction.

Form of measurement is just one way of classifying behaviour. Another classification system will be described in chapter 8 (characteristics of behaviour), but a general rule applies to both. When constructing or analysing a theory, one of the first things to do is to establish what kind of behaviour the theory is intended to explain. Any two theories *either* explain the same behaviour *or* explain different behaviours or different aspects of the same behaviour. In psychology there are many different kinds of behaviour which could be explained by a theory and as a consequence there may be many theories, each explaining either different or similar behaviours. When comparing theories it is therefore a useful exercise to establish first what the theories are intended to explain.

There are two basic questions which should be asked about a theory: 'What is the theory explaining' and 'How is the theory explaining it'. The first of these questions is answered by specifying the behaviour to be explained. In our initial discussion of theory construction it will be sufficient to answer the former question with respect to the form of measurement used to measure the behaviour.

The Situation

Situational factors are a class of concepts which are used to explain behaviour: situational factors, together with individual factors explain behaviour. Situational factors are sometimes referred to as stimuli; they are publicly observable events which happen to an individual. Situational factors can be classified in various ways. We shall use just one dichotomy: social situational factors and physical situational factors (Sherif and Sherif, 1969; Sells, 1963). Social situational factors consist of the effects of other people; physical situational factors refer to non-social aspects of the physical environment. Social situational factors make up a person's social environment; they include verbal statements from other people, non-verbal statements from other people, the mere presence of other people – any way in fact in which people can affect each other. Physical situational factors refer to physical events such as the weather, time of day and temperature, or any non-social way in which people can be affected by their environment. The social/physical distinction can be a useful one even though not all factors fall naturally into one or other of the two categories; it is a classification which is sometimes convenient, though not always unambiguous.

Some authors distinguish the *real* situation, which despite being theory laden is 'objectively' assessed by outside observers, from the *psychological* situation, which is how the situation is perceived by the individual who's behaviour is being explained. These authors argue that the latter, often referred to as 'the situation' provides better predictions of behaviour than the real situation (Koffka, 1935; Lewin, 1936, 1938). In this book the term situation refers to the real situation rather than the psychological situation. The psychological situation is a theoretical concept and the relation between the real and psychological situations will be examined as part of theory construction.

Processes

Psychologists use the word 'process' in different ways, but here we shall adopt just one specific meaning: a process is a sequence of events where some kind of prediction between events is possible. The distinguishing feature of a process is that the predictive sequence must entail some theoretically conceived elements or events which describe characteristics of the individual. A process must include at least one individual factor.

A theory consists of one or more processes. The events described in a process may entail any kind of individual characterisation. The term process is not limited, for example, to mechanistic descriptions. We shall not adopt the common practice of limiting the use of the term process to mechanistically conceived cognitive processes. A process is *any* predictive sequence which includes at least one individual factor.

Prediction or regularity of events does not happen by chance: there must be some reason for it. Where it is possible to predict one event from another, there must be some relation between the events which give rise to the ability to predict. This relation is called a causal relation. Prediction or regularity in events occurs *either* because there is a causal relation between the regularly occurring events *or* because there is a causal relation between each of the regularly occurring events and some common cause. The concept of a process is based on the idea that the events described in the process should be related by causal relations. The sequence is predictive because of causal relations between events in the sequence. In theoretical psychology the concept of cause is different from and more complex than the concept of cause as used in the natural sciences and will be discussed in chapter 5. In theoretical psychology the concept of cause is not limited to a mechanistic interpretation of cause and effect.

It is often useful to think of a causal relation in an abstracted sense of a function mapping between two sets

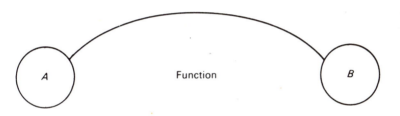

The function describes the form of the relation between *A* and *B*. Mathematically, there is no direction implied in the function. However, when the function describes a causal relation, we must introduce direction between the two sets. *A* causes *B*; the direction is from *A* to *B*.

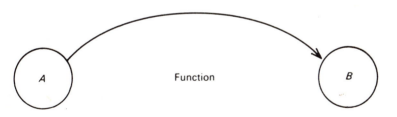

One interesting characteristic of the function relating two events is that it can be interpreted as an object. It is 'the thing which makes *A* cause *B*', but it is a different sort or 'level' of object from that which it relates. The use of a function as an object occurs but rarely in psychological theories. The best known example is the TOTE (Test-Operate-Test-Exit) heuristic of Miller, Galanter and Pribram (1960).

In the TOTE heuristic, an operator is something which effects a causal connection between two events or states. The concept of an operator has considerable theoretical interest and we shall discuss it in chapter 6. A process, then, consists of a series of events and functions or operators. The operators effect changes from one event to the next. The operators are a different order of concept from the events themselves, and it helps when conceptualising a process to keep the distinction clearly in mind. It should be noted that just as processes are not limited to a mechanistic interpretation, so the concept of an operator is not just limited to cause and effect relations between mechanistic events.

A process

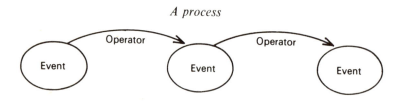

When explaining a phenomenon it is usual to describe a process which terminates in the occurrence of that phenomenon, that is, to describe a causally connected sequence of events occurring prior to the event to be explained. One end, the subsequent end, of the sequence consists of the event being explained. The other end, or antecedent end, is marked by some event which occurred previously, but it is not possible to specify how long ago or what the antecedent should consist of. It is possible to predict (and hence explain) an event from a number of different stages in the prior causal sequence. Imagine (to take the simplest example) a billiard ball which is rolling across the table and is going to hit another ball. One can predict the subsequent collision from any point in the billiard ball's path. One can focus on the point just before collision or on what was happening to the billiard ball way down at the other end of the table. In either case, one can predict from an antecedent event to the subsequent collision. In the same way, different stages of a causal sequence can be selected to explain the same event. The choice of one stage rather than another to explain an event is based on the internal characteristics of each explanation, in other words, that one explanation provides a more useful or useable explanation, that it provides a better insight or whatever.

Where two theories describe events at different stages leading up to a behaviour, then those theories are complementary rather than alternatives. They are complementary because the two theories taken together provide a more complete understanding of the processes underlying behaviour. Together, they may provide more precise prediction of the behaviour. Theories are complementary when they explain different stages of a sequence leading up to the same behaviour, but they can also be complementary for reasons to be discussed later. However, whatever the reason for theories being complementary, one objective in seeking a way of integrating theories is that through such integration different yet complementary theories can be placed in a more powerful overall explanatory framework. A second reason for seeking integration is that it enables us to compare and contrast alternative or competing explanations.

This chapter has served to introduce some of the concepts used in psychological theories. Observables such as the situation and behaviour have been distinguished from theoretical concepts. The ideas of process, cause and operators have been introduced. In the next few chapters some of these concepts will be examined in more depth and towards the end of the book (chapters 7 and 8) they will be tied together into a general integrative framework.

3 Hypothetical Constructs and Intervening Variables

Theoretical terms in psychology are used to describe characteristics of individuals. Of course, individuals can be described atheoretically: one can describe observable characteristics such as height, weight, or physiological response whilst making as few theoretical assumptions about these observables as possible. However, atheoretical characterisations of individuals are very limited and so when describing the individual it is common to make explicit theoretical assumptions. The observable characteristics are taken merely as indicators of the underlying theoretical concepts.

Theoretical concepts in psychology are generally referred to either as hypothetical constructs or as intervening variables. The difference between hypothetical constructs and intervening variables was defined by MacCorquodale and Meehl (1948). Nowadays their distinction is not always observed so that the meanings of the two terms are sometimes ambiguous. However, the terms will be used here in the sense originally defined by them, as they provide a useful conceptual distinction.

MacCorquodale and Meehl distinguish two sorts of theoretical term: those of an 'analytic' or 'abstractive' kind and those of an 'existential' or 'hypothetical' kind. They suggest the linguistic convention that the term *intervening variable* should be used for analytic or abstractive theoretical terms and the term *hypothetical construct* be used for existential or hypothetical theoretical terms. According to MacCorquodale and Meehl, intervening variables are identifiable by three characteristics.

First, the statement of such a concept does not contain any words which are not reducible to empirical laws.

Second, the validity of the empirical laws is both necessary and sufficient for the "correctness" of the statements about the concept.

Third, the quantitative expression of the concept can be obtained without mediate inference by suitable groupings of terms in the quantitative empirical laws.   (p. 107).

The term hypothetical construct, on the other hand, should be used for theoretical terms of an existential or hypothetical nature.

Their formulation involves words not wholly reducible to the words in the empirical laws; the validity of the empirical laws is not a sufficient condition for the truth of the concept, in as much as it contains surplus meaning; and the quantitative form of the concept is not obtainable simply by grouping empirical terms and functions.   (p. 107).

The fundamental difference between hypothetical constructs and intervening variables is that hypothetical constructs refer to things which actually exist; intervening variables refer to things which do not exist, they merely refer to abstractions from data. Mac-Corquodale and Meehl are not clear about *how* hypothetical constructs are supposed to exist. The implication of their 1948 paper is that hypothetical constructs should have some form of physiological representation and hence exist in the same way that nerves exist. However, later, Cronback and Meehl (1955) correct 'certain excesses' of the earlier paper and suggest that physiological representation is just one way in which hypothetical constructs can exist, presumably there being other ways – though what they are is not elucidated. For the moment it will be assumed that hypothetical constructs have some form of existential status, and the question of the nature of that status will be considered in the next chapter.

An intervening variable is an abstraction from a measure of behaviour, nothing more. When one says that 'intelligence is what intelligence tests measure' then the concept of intelligence is being treated as an intervening variable. The concept is defined as the result of a particular measurement procedure, it is an abstraction from data and exists only to the extent that the data exist. However, if one takes the approach that 'intelligence tests measure intelligence', then intelligence is being treated as a hypothetical construct. If intelligence tests measure intelligence, then intelligence exists independently of the test. The test gives an approximation of the extent of intelligence, but the test does not define intelligence in that the concept of intelligence entails something more than just the test.

The set of measures which define an intervening variable are called operations, and so an intervening variable is *operationally defined*. In practice, an intervening variable is defined by a set of behaviours, that is, behaviour carried out by the individual whose intervening variables are to be defined. The description of a hypothetical construct should entail an account of the operations or behaviours likely to be associated with that concept, but an account of the operations associated with the concept does not fully describe the hypothetical construct. A hypothetical construct can be operational-ised but not operationally defined. Some of the meaning embodied in a hypothetical construct cannot be described by listing that construct's operations.

Hypothetical constructs contain 'surplus meaning' (Mac-Corquodale and Meehl, 1948), that is, meaning which cannot be expressed by simply listing a concept's operations. A hypothetical construct is not just a list of operations, as it has an existence which is independent of the operations. A hypothetical construct is actually there (though in what sense it is actually there we reserve until later) even though it may not be manifesting any or all of its behavioural consequences. Although one can provide a list of operations associated with a hypothetical construct, that list is in principle incomplete as there may be additional operations attached to the concept which have not yet been discovered. The surplus meaning attached to the concept cannot be defined exactly. It is possible to give a representation of surplus meaning, but the surplus meaning is not exactly the same as the analogue. A hypothetical construct is therefore an 'open concept' (Tuomela, 1973), that is, a concept which cannot be defined analytically. In practice this has the effect that the meaning of a hypothetical construct cannot be detailed exactly: hypothetical constructs have fuzzy conceptual boundaries, interven-ing variables are absolutely precise concepts with precise boundaries. There is no possibility of ambiguity in the description of an intervening variable as its description simply entails listing its operations. However, there is the possibility of ambiguity in the description of a hypothetical construct. The hallmark of neobehav-iourist explanations is that theoretical terms should be limited to operationally defined theoretical terms, that is, limited to intervening variables. The advantage of such a limitation is quite obvious: the more ambiguous and less precise kind of theoretical term is avoided.

Hypothetical constructs and intervening variables are true in different ways. Intervening variables are true by virtue of correct definition; their truth is not established by empirical testing. To say that operations x, y, and z define intervening variable Q, is to say that Q is the measure of operations x, y, and z. Q would only be false if some other incorrect measures or operations with which to assess Q were used. Hypothetical constructs, on the other hand, are not true by virtue of correct definition. The truth of a hypothetical construct is evaluated by empirical observation, by seeing whether events in the world lead one to conclude that that hypothetical construct should exist. Imagine that there is an object in a room made with translucent walls and that the shadow of the object falls on the walls. Depending on the shape of the shadow we draw certain conclusions about the object within the room, though we can never be certain that our conclusions are correct for we can never get inside the room. So it is with hypothetical constructs in psychology. One sees the shadow of hypothetical constructs in the behaviour of people; but although certain conclusions about these hypothetical constructs can be drawn from an observation of behaviour, one can never be certain that the conclusions are correct. The truth of a hypothetical construct can never be established with absolute certainty; one can never be certain that the object referred to by the hypothetical construct actually exists.

Some people might consider this difference between hypothetical constructs and intervening variables to the disadvantage of hypothetical constructs, since the truth of the latter always remains uncertain. Nowadays, the consensus of opinion amongst many psychologists and philosophers of science is that there is too high a price to pay for the convenience and unambiguity of operationally defined theoretical terms and one should instead accept non-operationally defined terms. Therefore the advantages of hypothetical constructs – or existential theoretical terms – should be considered to see why some people consider them attractive. Before doing so the position so far ought to be summarised. Three approaches to explanation have been distinguished.

(a) An atheoretical approach where no form of theoretical term is allowed in an explanation. The disadvantage of such radical behaviourism was discussed in chapter 1.

(*b*) A theoretical approach where theoretical terms are limited to operationally defined terms or intervening variables, an approach usually associated with neobehaviourism.

(*c*) A theoretical approach where theoretical terms are not limited to intervening variables but will include both hypothetical constructs and intervening variables, or just hypothetical constructs.

In chapter 1 several advantages of the theoretical approach to explanation were discussed. One advantage was that theories provide an account of underlying causes; another was the ability of a theory to summarise a large amount of data within a single theoretical statement; and another was the observation that theories often act as a heuristic for guiding empirical research. These advantages are realised better by hypothetical constructs than by intervening variables.

The fundamental difference between hypothetical constructs and intervening variables is that hypothetical constructs refer to things that actually exist (or at least they are assumed to exist) whereas intervening variables are just an abstraction from data. Because they exist, the objects referred to by hypothetical constructs can affect or influence or cause each other. Intervening variables, on the other hand, cannot affect each other because intervening variables do not exist beyond an abstraction from the empirical laws. An intervening variable is just an abstraction from data which intervenes, as a concept, in a stimulus–response link up. It does not have causal properties. If an explanation is to be limited to intervening variables, then for any explanation (that is, the prediction of a particular behaviour) there can be just one intervening variable which helps predict the response from the stimulus. If hypothetical constructs are admitted to an explanation, however, then any explanation may involve many different hypothetical constructs which interact with each other. It would be possible, for example, to postulate a causal chain of hypothetical constructs, or some other more complex interactive system. Thus, if one wishes to describe the processes underlying behaviour, hypothetical constructs must be used and not intervening variables, because only hypothetical constructs have the causal properties necessary to describe a process. Because of their existential status, hypothetical constructs can be given theoretical properties or functions which cannot be ascribed to intervening variables.

Both hypothetical constructs and intervening variables have the property of summarising data, but hypothetical constructs can provide a more general summary than intervening variables. An intervening variable is itself a device for expressing or summarising data, but it is only a device for summarising a particular, predetermined, set of data. Data is also summarised in the operations of a hypothetical construct but the summary of data is not restricted to a particular set of operations. Because a hypothetical construct can manifest itself in different ways it can summarise a much wider and potentially limitless range of data. The predictions made by an intervening variable are limited to the set of operations defining the intervening variable. Theories incorporating intervening variables are therefore poor at providing new empirical ideas and guiding further empirical research. Hypothetical constructs on the other hand, contain surplus meaning and the surplus meaning is an excellent source for generating novel predictions. The 'openness' and speculative nature of hypothetical constructs, the fact that they contain surplus meaning makes them potentially excellent concepts for generating new empirical ideas.

One of the characteristics of surplus meaning is that it is never absolutely precise, it cannot be defined exactly. The advantage theories have of guiding and stimulating new empirical research is only achieved when the theoretical concepts are speculative and slightly vague. Although too much conceptual openness leads to low predictive power and an inability to integrate research, if one tries to achieve complete precision then some of the advantages of introducing theoretical terms is lost. The amount of conceptual openness must be regulated. A little conceptual openness is allowable, a moderate openness in the theoretical concepts, but this openness must never increase to such an extent that it disrupts the efficient functioning of theories.

Construct validity

Because the object referred to by a hypothetical construct actually exists, it is possible to make predictions about data which go beyond the original listing of the operations which form part of the description of the hypothetical construct. In practice, this means that one can obtain evidence for the existence of a hypothetical construct in different ways. Different kinds of data will be capable of giving different 'sightings' onto the same hypothetical construct. The more observations there are which are consistent with the hypothetical construct, the more confident one can feel that the construct is true, and thus the greater the construct validity. The validity of a construct is best established when the evidence for the construct comes from many different kinds of source, that is, when one obtains different sightings onto the hypothetical construct. When evidence for a hypothetical construct comes from many different sorts of data, some perhaps experimental and some non-experimental, then there are good grounds for attributing validity to the construct because the consistent yet disparate effects imply the existence of a hypothetical construct manifesting itself in different ways. Note that the incentive to look for different sightings is based on the assumption that the object referred to by a hypothetical construct really exists and therefore manifests itself in different ways.

A well-known example of constructs being validated from different sorts of data is the extraversion/introversion personality dimension proposed by Eysenck. The dimension extraversion/introversion has been described in terms of cortical excitation. However, there is also evidence, from factor analytic studies with questionnaire data, that a personality factor exists which is consistent with the hypothesis of excitation. There is also experimental evidence for the dimension: extraverts (identified from questionnaires) perform differently from introverts on certain tasks and the differences are consistent with differences in cortical excitation. Of course, the extraversion/introversion dimension may not exist. The evidence may be just a combination of artifact and chance findings but one positive aspect in its favour is that the evidence for the construct comes not from one, but from a number of different sorts of data, and it is this multiplicity of evidence which increases confidence in the validity of the construct.

The study of psychology is sometimes divided into two forms, nomothetic psychology and ideographic psychology. Nomothetic psychology explains differences between groups where the different groups have been subjected to different kinds of experimental treatment. Ideographic psychology is concerned with individual differences. (The distinction is not entirely satisfactory.) Underwood (1975) has suggested that these different approaches can provide a useful heuristic for construct validation. Hypothetical constructs

which are postulated to explain some differences in group performance do not cease to exist when individual differences are studied.
Underwood suggests that whenever a mechanism or process is
postulated to account for some findings in nomothetic psychology,
then that process or mechanism may vary between individuals and
one should look for such individual differences as further evidence for
the construct's existence. 'If we include in our nomothetic theories a
process or mechanism that can be measured reliably outside of the
situation for which it is serving its theoretical purpose, we have an
immediate test of the validity of the theoretical formulation . . .'
Underwood indeed goes so far as to recommend that when one
explains differences in group performance one should try to postulate
hypothetical constructs which can easily be measured from the point
of view of individual differences, but this suggestion seems to be
unnecessarily restrictive. However, one can certainly recommend
that when a hypothetical construct is postulated to explain some
aspect of behaviour which is investigated under standard experimental conditions, then the validity of the hypothetical construct will be
strengthened by taking another sighting from the point of view of
individual differences.

Explanatory fictions

One of the arguments used by Skinner against the introduction of
theoretical terms is that they create explanatory fictions, that they
merely constitute a redescription of the behaviour. If one says, for
example, that a person is smiling because he is happy, then the
attribution of happiness tells one nothing more about the person's
smiling behaviour than the simple description of the behaviour. Or
does it? One of the characteristics of hypothetical constructs is that
they can go beyond the original listing of operations to predict new
observations. If the dispositional characteristic of happiness is used
to predict new behaviour which could not be predicted by simply
knowing that the person was smiling, then the concept is not a mere
fiction, it is a useful predictive tool. Explanatory fictions occur when
theories are very simple; they occur when a theoretical concept is
introduced merely to explain one behaviour, or one kind of stimulus –
response linkage. In the case of such simple theories it is certainly
worth questioning whether there is any point in introducing the
theoretical term. Theoretical terms prove their worth when they are

used in more complex theories, and in particular when they provide predictions in areas which, on the basis of the behaviour alone, are not obviously related. However, this is a characteristic of hypothetical constructs rather than intervening variables.

Theoretical terms can be eliminated *after* one has established the data, but they cannot be eliminated before. The principal argument for the use of theoretical terms is that they predict ahead of data, they are tools for guiding scientific *discovery*. Underwood makes the suggestion that when constructing a theory, the theory should include at least two theoretical concepts which are capable of interacting with each other, that is, at least two hypothetical constructs which are capable of interacting with each other. The rationale behind Underwood's stipulation is that by introducing this element of complexity into a theory the criticism that the theoretical concepts constitute an explanatory fiction are avoided. When hypothetical constructs interact, they are likely to lead to complex and varied predictions which are not limited to a single behaviour.

Using hypothetical constructs and intervening variables

It was intimated at the beginning of this chapter that the difference between hypothetical constructs and intervening variables (that is, between existential and abstractive concepts) is not always fully appreciated. The point is that it is actually more convenient to be dealing with an intervening variable when one is running an experiment, but more convenient to deal with a hypothetical construct when theorising. If the dependent variable in an experiment is treated as an intervening variable, then there is no problem about construct validity as the measure and the concept are one. It is very convenient to be able to say 'For the purposes of this experiment, concept X will be defined by measure Y' and it is, of course, perfectly legitimate to do so. However, one should not go on from there to theorise about concept X as though it were a hypothetical construct; hypothetical constructs having the useful theoretical property of causality. Any desire to have one's cake and eat – to have an intervening variable in an experiment and a hypothetical construct in a theory – must be strongly resisted, otherwise one draws false conclusions about theory from experiments.

It is essential that description of concepts in an experimental setting correspond to the same description in a theoretical setting. If a concept is defined operationally as a set of measures obtained in an experiment, then any conclusions drawn about the experiment are peculiar to that particular measure of the concept. Results should not be generalised to other measures. On the other hand, if one introduces a theory involving hypothetical constructs, then any experimental measure of that hypothetical construct is an indirect approximation of the hypothetical construct. One can never measure a hypothetical construct with absolute certainty. However, given adequate construct validity, the results of such an experiment can be generalised to experiments involving other measures of the same hypothetical construct. Depending on whether one treats theoretical terms as intervening variables or hypothetical constructs, one can draw different kinds of conclusions from experimental data. The difference between hypothetical constructs and intervening variables must be made explicit if the meaning of theoretical terms is to be used and communicated correctly.

4 The Nature of Hypothetical Constructs

So far in this book the word hypothetical construct has been used for a particular sort of theoretical concept which is found in psychology. Philosophers of science (for example, Geach and Black, 1970) maintain that words describing concepts should be different from the words describing the objects or entities to which the concepts refer. In this and later chapters entities as well as concepts in psychology will be examined. So, to make the concept–object distinction clear with respect to hypothetical constructs the form 'hypothetical construct' will now be used to denote the theoretical concept, and hypothetical construct to denote the theoretical entity.

A 'hypothetical construct' is a theoretical concept: it refers to something which cannot be seen. In order to describe a hypothetical construct we therefore have to refer to things which can be seen, things which are publicly observable. 'Hypothetical constructs' can only acquire meaning by reference to something we already know about; so the meaning of the unobservable hypothetical construct is described and communicated by finding observable characteristics and events which can act as an analogy of the theoretical construct. This observable analogy illustrates what the unobservable hypothetical construct is like. Thus, 'hypothetical constructs' are described by linking the 'hypothetical construct' with observables: the sentences which link the theoretical terms to statements in an observation vocabulary are usually called correspondence rules. Correspondence rules are sentences which relate the theoretical concept to publicly observable characteristics and events. Correspondence rules may include some of the sentences which are used to describe a theory in which the theoretical concept appears.

When discussing the meaning of a 'hypothetical construct' it is often helpful to consider the correspondence rules which provide the concept with its meaning. Correspondence rules in psychology are slightly different from correspondence rules found in other disciplines. In the physical sciences the observables incorporated into correspondence rules form one undifferentiated category, the category called by Carnap 'thing language' or the everyday language of object description. In psychology, on the other hand, the observables incorporated into the correspondence rules fall into discrete categories and, as will be seen, the use of different kinds of observable in the correspondence rules leads to different kinds of 'hypothetical construct'.

In the previous chapter it was established that the description of a 'hypothetical construct' should include an account of the operations as well as the surplus meaning embodied in the concept. These two aspects of a 'hypothetical construct' constitute two descriptive components: an *operational* component, which provides an account of the operations associated with the concept, and a *nature* component which, amongst other things, provides an account of the surplus meaning embodied in the concept. Loosely speaking, the operational component describes what the concept does; the nature component describes what the concept is. A full description of a 'hypothetical construct' must include both components.

THE OPERATIONAL COMPONENT

Every hypothetical construct has behavioural consequences. In other words, the hypothetical construct affects behaviour in one way or another. The behavioural consequences constitute the operational component of the 'hypothetical construct'. The operational component consists of a list of behavioural consequences or operations associated with the 'hypothetical construct'. The correspondence rules which provide the operational component with meaning do so by referring to the observable *behaviour*; behaviour, that is, of the organism whose behaviour is being described. In that there are different kinds or descriptions of behaviour, the operational component can be described in different ways. However, the general principle of using observable behaviour to give meaning to the operational component of the 'hypothetical construct' remains the same. As all 'hypothetical constructs' entail an operational component, the description of all 'hypothetical constructs' must include a description of the behavioural consequences associated with that 'hypothetical construct'. This is an important rule: all 'hypothetical constructs' must be clearly related to behaviour in terms of behavioural consequences.

There are a number of different kinds of behavioural description which can be used in the correspondence rules of the operational component. One major difference between these different forms of description is whether or not some form of statistical abstraction is employed. In some cases, the operational component is specified by listing the behaviours which are consequent on that 'hypothetical construct'. For example, one might say that the 'hypothetical construct' 'achievement motive' is associated with the extent of achievement orientated behaviours such as 'economic success', 'perseverance on a task', and 'achievement imagery as measured on the TAT'. Alternatively, the description of the operational component may involve a statistical abstraction from a set of behaviours. For example, Cattel (1965) defines personality dimensions on the basis of a statistical abstraction (factor analysis) from responses to items in a questionnaire. In the case of Cattel's personality dimensions, no particular behaviour is associated with the 'hypothetical construct', rather, it is the overall pattern of behaviours which give the operational component its particular meaning. A 'hypothetical construct' may be associated with any kind of operation or combination of operations. There are no restrictions; behavioural description both with and without statistical abstraction may be employed together.

Much of the meaning of the operational component derives from the way in which the 'hypothetical construct' is used in theories. Where a theory entails many interacting hypothetical constructs, then the meaning of the operational component of a 'hypothetical construct' must be understood in terms of the behavioural consequences of the interacting system as a whole. The operational component of hypothetical constructs which interact with other hypothetical constructs must be examined in terms of the concept of *function*.

When describing the function of an object, one is describing the consequences the object has within a system of other objects. Functions are always described in terms of a system or conceptual framework: *functions do not exist independently of systems*. This is an important point. When describing the function of an object, the system within which the object acts is often not specified; this failure arises because the system is usually self-evident. In psychology, however, theoretical concepts can function in different systems and so it becomes necessary to specify to which system a function refers.

A hypothetical construct has two functions. First it can have the function of causing behaviour; in this case the function is located in a system of behaviours. Second, a hypothetical construct can have the function of causing change amongst other hypothetical constructs; in this case the function is located in a system of hypothetical constructs. Although these two different sorts of function can be separated conceptually, in practice they are inter-related. They are inter-related because *all* hypothetical constructs have behavioural consequences, they all have the function of causing behaviour. In order to understand the operations of a hypothetical construct which interacts with other hypothetical constructs its functioning in relation to other hypothetical constructs must also be understood. When describing the operations of a 'hypothetical construct' which features in a complex interactive theory, it is therefore necessary to elucidate the functional characteristics of the 'hypothetical construct' in relation to other theoretical concepts.

THE NATURE COMPONENT

The operational component of a 'hypothetical construct' has never presented psychologists with too much of a problem. The operational component, after all, is similar in some respects to the conceptually simpler intervening variable. The nature component, on the other hand, has always been a bit of a puzzle and psychologists have generally avoided discussing it. When specific attempts have been made to analyse the nature component, they are not very convincing (see, for example Harré and Secord's 'psycho-physical mix').

It is important to establish what is meant by the nature component of a hypothetical construct and how it is used. The nature component provides the *ontological status* of the hypothetical construct; it indicates in what sense the hypothetical construct exists. Not only does the nature component indicate how the hypothetical construct exists, but in doing so it provides the researcher with a source of surplus meaning. The nature component provides a link with a set of hypotheses or heuristics which psychologists can use to generate new empirical ideas. If the nature component is not examined, then one might as well limit oneself to intervening variables, as many of the advantages of a hypothetical construct stem from the nature component.

In order to understand the nature component, the way in which 'hypothetical constructs' acquire meaning, that is, the correspondence rules, must be considered again. Some correspondence rules refer to behaviour (an observable) and these correspondence rules provide the concept with its operational component. However, other observables are also introduced into correspondence rules and it is the correspondence rules using these other, non-behaviour, observables which provide the nature component with meaning.

A hypothetical construct can have one of three different natures. In other words it can have one of three different kinds of ontological status. Different kinds of correspondence rule are used to describe each of these different kinds of nature. Correspondence rules entail reference to observables and broadly speaking the observables incorporated into the different kinds of correspondence rule fall into three separate categories. The three different natures or kinds of ontological status of a hypothetical construct are *physiological, mentalistic* and *mechanistic*. That is, there are physiological hypothetical constructs, mentalistic hypothetical constructs and mechanistic hypothetical constructs.

Physiological hypothetical constructs

Of the three kinds of hypothetical construct, physiological hypothetical constructs are the most straightforward since they have the same nature as theoretical entities found in other disciplines. It is possible to explain behaviour by referring to the brain (or any other relevant organ) of the behaving individual. Such explanations employ a microanalysis of the brain, that is, they refer to the small unobservable parts or characteristics of the brain, and the results of this microanalysis constitute physiological hypothetical constructs. Examples of physiological hypothetical constructs are neurones and transmitter substances.

Physiological 'hypothetical constructs', like other 'hypothetical constructs', are described by correspondence rules which refer to observables. The observables used in the description of physiological 'hypothetical constructs', like the observables used in the description of theoretical concepts in other disciplines, comprise a ragbag of everyday observation or 'thing language' (Carnap, 1938). Reference is sometimes made to macroscopic physiological structures; sometimes to physical inorganic structures. By referring to these observables an analogy of the physiological hypothetical construct is built up; the physiological hypothetical construct is described by providing an observable analogy. The difference between the physiological hypothetical construct and the analogy is simply that the physiological hypothetical construct is usually much smaller than the analogy and may consist of different chemical substances.

One important characteristic of physiological hypothetical constructs is that they exist in space. Physiological hypothetical constructs are real objects like tables and chairs and they have the same ontological status as any other physical object. A second characteristic of physiological hypothetical constructs is that, like theoretical entities in other disciplines, they exist on a continuum of observability. A neurone, for example, is more observable than a transmitter substance. Both these characteristics distinguish physiological hypothetical constructs from mentalistic or mechanistic hypothetical constructs. Mentalistic and mechanistic hypothetical constructs do not exist in space and cannot be described as existing in a continuum of observability.

The nature component of a physiological hypothetical construct provides a description of a microphysiological object; the operational component specifies some of the behavioural consequences of this microphysiological object. The two components are related: particular characteristics of the nature tend to have particular behavioural consequences. For example the structure of neurones is such that they have a refractory period and as a consequence certain fast oscillating stimuli are not perceived to oscillate. It is this relationship between the nature and operational components which is important for generating new empirical ideas or new behavioural consequences. By using knowledge or by hypothesising about the nature of a particular hypothetical construct one can make inferences about likely behavioural consequences. New empirical research can then be set up to test these new ideas. Thus, the nature of a physiological 'hypothetical construct' acts as a heuristic for generating new empirical research.

Mentalistic hypothetical constructs

In everyday language, mentalistic hypothetical constructs are called 'thoughts' or 'experiences' or 'phenomena' or 'the contents of the mind'. Although the contents of consciousness are not publicly observable (and hence defined as unobservable) they are open to private scrutiny and such private scrutiny has led to a set of (publicly) observable statements or words corresponding to those private events. Private and unobservable mental states are described by referring to publicly observable words which are conventionally associated with particular mind states. The statements which describe mental states are correspondence rules since they link an observable word with an unobservable mental state which someone has experienced. The experience is a theoretical entity: it is a mentalistic hypothetical construct.

Ever since the first psychological laboratory was opened in 1879 by Wundt, psychologists have studied aspects of the mind. Much of the early work carried out by Wundt and his associates was concerned with classifying sensations and analysing them into their constituent components. For instance, he distinguished sensations, images, ideas and feelings and studied these different mental contents using a combination of introspection and experimentation. Other psychologists (for example, James, Brentano) disputed that sensations could be broken down into components and studied them from a holistic point of view, and this holistic approach to studying sensations was later associated with phenomenology. Later work focusses on more complex aspects of the mind. For example, Köhler (1947), Peters (1958) and Harré and Secord (1972), have examined the introspected accounts or the reasons people give for their actions. These authors suggest that behaviour can be explained by reference to the thoughts of the person engaged in that behaviour, a suggestion which forms one of the assumptions of modern attribution theory. Yet another approach focusses on the constructs (Kelly, 1955), or on the judgemental dimensions (Osgood, Suci and Tannenbaum, 1957) which people use to understand the world they live in, both of which can also be used to explain behaviour.

One way of using thoughts or mentalistic concepts is to treat them as theoretical concepts or mentalistic 'hypothetical constructs' which are used in theories explaining behaviour. Mentalistic 'hypothetical constructs' have the capacity to explain behaviour because they can be shown to be associated with particular patterns of behavioural response. One can predict from thought to behaviour. By knowing the mental state of an individual (and by knowing the situation he is in) it is possible to predict what he will do next. Thus, theories which include mentalistic 'hypothetical constructs' can be used to explain behaviour.

Often the relationship between mental state and behaviour is partially known through everyday experience – everyone notices relationships between thoughts and behaviour – but a more accurate picture of the behavioural consequences of mental states can be built up by suitable empirical techniques. The relationship between mental states and behaviour need not be self-evident; although one may be able to explain behaviour by using mental concepts, it does not necessarily follow that behaviour can be explained by common sense.

Mentalistic hypothetical constructs have a different kind of ontological status from that of physiological hypothetical constructs. Physiological hypothetical constructs exist in space; mentalistic hypothetical constructs do not. Mentalistic hypothetical constructs exist as a set of experiences which an individual could have. Various circumstances 'activate' these experiences and the particular experience can then be introspected. Mentalistic hypothetical constructs are thoughts; they exist not as objects in the physical world but as private experiences which can be described by individuals having those experiences.

The fact that everyone has private experiences, the fact that particular experiences lead to particular behaviour, means that one can draw on one's own experience to generate new empirical ideas. The nature of the mentalistic hypothetical construct, that is what the thought actually 'feels' like, acts as a heuristic for generating new empirical ideas, ideas which should then be tested in the usual manner. However, it is important to distinguish an intuitive understanding of people from testable statements involving mentalistic 'hypothetical constructs'. The intuitive understanding is capable of generating testable statements but until those testable statements are actually formulated the intuitive understanding does not constitute a scientific explanation, even though it may provide a useful adjunct to theory construction. Ability to empathise with other people, for example, is a *source* of empirical ideas involving mentalistic 'hypothetical constructs' but the empathy is not itself a scientific explanation. Once generated the empirical statements exist independently and can be communicated independently of the ability to empathise with others. Empathic understanding, however, is usually not testable and can only be communicated to others with similar empathic ability.

Although it is usual to equate mentalistic hypothetical constructs with conscious thoughts or conscious mental states, some authors have suggested that unconscious thoughts or mental states exist. Unconscious thoughts are similar to their conscious counterparts in that they are described in much the same way. That is, the correspondence rules describing unconscious thoughts are the same as those describing conscious thoughts, with the sole difference that the introspecting subject is supposed to be unaware of the unconscious thoughts. Unconscious mentalistic hypothetical constructs have one less behavioural consequence than conscious mentalistic hypothetical constructs: people are not able to report unconscious thoughts, and so it is more difficult to establish their presence. Because the existence of unconscious mentalistic hypothetical constructs is more difficult to establish than the presence of conscious mentalistic hypothetical constructs, some authors reject the use of unconscious mentalistic hypothetical constructs, rejecting them either on the basis that they do not suppose unconscious mental states to exist, or because they do not consider unconscious mental states to constitute a useful explanatory concept. However, other authors, particularly those with a psychoanalytic orientation, suggest that a consideration of unconscious mental states is indispensable for explaining certain kinds of behaviour. Although there is no overriding reason for rejecting unconscious mentalistic hypothetical constructs, it is evident that they should only be used if they lead to theories with good explanatory power.

Mechanistic hypothetical constructs

Hypothetical constructs are sometimes described by reference to mechanical systems, or in other words by reference to mechanisms which happen in the world of observable physical events. For example, one approach to explaining aggressive behaviour is to suggest that aggression, a hypothetical construct, builds up like water in a tank and the aggression, like the water, must somehow be released. Behaviour in attention or decision-making tasks is often explained in terms of selectors, filters and buffer stores, all of which can be identified as parts of a mechanical or mechanical/electrical system. Such explanations employ concepts which are linked to mechanisms. The correspondence rules describing these mechanistic 'hypothetical constructs' refer to parts of mechanical systems.

Although Freud was one of the first to employ mechanistic concepts (for example, conservation of psychic energy) at the beginning of the century, the rationale for introducing mechanistic description in psychology stems from the work of Craik (1943). Craik argues that the nervous system should be 'viewed as a calculating machine, capable of paralleling or modelling external events' and suggests 'that this process of paralleling is the basic feature of thought and explanation' (p. 121). Craik argues that the brain must be able to anticipate events in the outside world, and so the nervous system must, in some way, be able to follow or model (in the correct sense of isomorphism) the events in the external world. Psychological explanation should therefore entail the same mechanical concepts which are found in the physical world, and explanations which treat these mechanical events 'as if' they were actually occurring will thereby give an explanation of the processes underlying behaviour.

In 1958, Broadbent popularised the use of mechanistic 'hypothetical constructs' for explanations in cognitive psychology. Broadbent can be considered to be the originator of the now familiar kind of explanation which consists of 'boxes' joined by 'arrows' where the boxes represent mechanistic concepts and the arrows represent a transition from one concept to the next. Further justification for the use of mechanistic concepts comes from the work of Deutsch (1960) and Fodor (1968), whose arguments have been labelled the 'hardware thesis' (Gendron, 1971).

Fodor suggests that mechanistic explanations (actually he says psychological explanations, but his argument only applies to explanations involving mechanistic 'hypothetical constructs') provide an account of the *functions* of the nervous system. Physiology shows what the physiological parts consist of, but psychology shows what the parts do. Physiology provides a structural account of the brain, mechanistic concepts provide a functional characterisation of those structures. Although structures and functions are statistically related they are not logically related, they are not one and the same thing. Consider, for example, a car engine. The word 'camshaft' describes a structure; the word 'valve lifter' describes a function. Camshafts usually have the function of 'lifting valves'. If we wish to discover which part of an engine acts as a valve lifter then we would probably be correct to search for a structure that looks like a camshaft. However, there are other ways of lifting valves which do not involve structures resembling a camshaft. Conversely, when we see a camshaft then we are likely to think that the function of that object is to lift valves; but it may not be; the camshaft may in fact be part of a modern sculpture and have the function of stimulating one's aesthetic sense. Although structure and function are statistically related, it is not possible to deduce structures from functions and *vice versa*.

Fodor uses this distinction between structure and function as an argument against the reduction of psychology to physiology. Reductionism usually involves a microanalysis of one discipline by another; that is the reducing discipline analyses the parts of the reduced discipline. Psychology provides a functional analysis of the structures described by physiology. Physiology does not describe the parts of psychology and so psychology cannot be microanalysed by physiology. As Fodor puts it succintly 'Pains do not have parts, so brain cells are not parts of pains' (p. 112).

The hardware thesis has been criticised by Gendron (1971) on the grounds that physiology does not just provide a description of the structure of the brain (as would be the case of anatomy), it also provides information about the function of the brain. A little consideration will show that this is in fact the case: physiology does provide an account of function.

The difference between Fodor and Gendron arises over the use of the word function. As was said earlier, functions do not exist independently of systems; when the function of an object is described, it should be done by specifying the system within which the object functions. Hypothetical constructs have two functions: the first is that of explaining behaviour, and in this respect both physiological and mechanistic (and indeed mentalistic) hypothetical constructs are similar; the second function is that of interacting with other hypothetical constructs. It is this second, interactive, function in which physiological and mechanistic hypothetical constructs differ, and they differ because the functions are located in different systems. They are located in a system of physiological activity and mechanism respectively. In a sense, Fodor is correct. Mechanistic 'hypothetical constructs' do provide a functional characterisation of physiological structures. However, the functional characterisation provided by those mechanistic 'hypothetical constructs' is different from the functional characterisation which is also provided by the physiological structures. The physiological and mechanistic functions are located in different systems. The reason for using mechanistic 'hypothetical constructs' stems from the idea that these non-physiological, mechanistic functional characterisations form a useful explanatory tool.

Although some of the features of mechanistic hypothetical constructs have just been described their ontological status has not been established. The key to understanding the nature of mechanistic hypothetical constructs lies not with their relationship to physiological structures but with their relationship to physical mechanisms. After all, the observables used in correspondence rules describing mechanistic 'hypothetical constructs' consist of physical mechanisms and not physiological structures. The nature of mechanistic hypothetical constructs must therefore be related in some way to physical mechanisms.

When mechanistic concepts are introduced into an explanation, it is not supposed that little boxes or whatever exist somewhere in the brain, but it is expected that behaviour can be explained by introducing mechanistic concepts 'as if' the physical structures they refer to existed. These 'as if' mechanistic structures are not located in real physical space, but exist as an entirely hypothetical group of concepts having all the properties of their physical counterparts. The properties will include physical location in an 'as if' space, conservation of 'as if' energy and so on. Mechanistic hypothetical concepts exist because we treat the mechanical structures 'as if' they really existed when we explain behaviour: their ontological status is that of hypothetical 'as if' mechanical structures.

The functional characteristics of a mechanistic hypothetical construct can be deduced (they are exactly equivalent) from the functional characteristics of the real-life physical object which is used to describe that hypothetical construct. Of course, the list of functional characteristics associated with a physical object is in principle incomplete (because it is an open concept) and it is always possible to generate new functional characteristics by using knowledge of the relationship between physical structure and what that structure can do. In generating these new ideas new functional characteristics (which include behavioural consequences) are provided for the mechanistic hypothetical construct. Thus it is possible to use the nature of the mechanistic hypothetical construct, that is, its relationship with physical mechanisms, to generate new empirical ideas.

IDENTITY RELATIONS

It has been suggested that three separate kinds of hypothetical construct should be distinguished, each kind having a different ontological status. Why should this be so? Why not have just one kind of hypothetical construct which simultaneously has mechanistic, mentalistic and physiological ontological status? After all, some hypothetical constructs do seem to have this combined ontological status. The reason for suggesting that the three different kinds of hypothetical construct should be separated is that it provides a clearer and less potentially ambiguous formulation of theoretical concepts. There are many different systematisations of 'hypothetical constructs' which could be devised, but the recommendation of one systematisation over another depends on the internal properties of the explanations thereby provided: systematisations of theoretical concepts are not true or false, they are just more or less useful. There are two reasons why a conceptual separation of the three kinds of hypothetical construct should provide a more useful and less ambiguous classification system of 'hypothetical constructs'. First, it draws attention to the nature of the concepts being used, and it will be argued later that the nature of a 'hypothetical construct' forms the basis for understanding causality between hypothetical constructs. Second, not all hypothetical constructs are used as though they have mechanistic, mentalistic and physiological ontological status simultaneously, and so a separation of these three different kinds of ontological status allows an appropriate distinction to be made. In fact, the distinction of three different kinds of hypothetical construct provides a classification system which is consistent with much of the current use of theoretical concepts in psychology.

Although a conceptual separation of three different kinds of hypothetical construct can be made, it happens sometimes that hypothetical constructs of differing ontological status appear to be related. For instance, a mechanistic concept may entail a particular kind of functional characterisation of part of the nervous system; a form of neurological activity may be correlated with particular sensations; a mechanistic concept may be associated with a particular sensation. Although such relationships are not very common they are by no means rare. For example, noradrenaline depletion and the feeling of depression are sometimes correlated; Shallice (1972) suggests that consciousness should be associated with certain parts of a mechanistic system. Research on arousal has used the idea of a relationship between physiological activity in parts of the nervous system and an arousal component in a mechanistic system.

The relationship between 'hypothetical constructs' of differing ontological status is determined by the *operational* component of the concepts. When the operational components of two 'hypothetical constructs' are defined as being identical, then those two hypothetical constructs are said to be *identified*. When two 'hypothetical constructs' are supposed to have the same operations, that is to have the same behavioural consequences, then it is probable that the two 'hypothetical constructs' refer to the same event or 'thing' which is responsible for those operations. When 'hypothetical constructs' are identified then it can be said that the theoretical concepts are *different descriptions of the same event*. Any event can be described in different ways: a blind man may describe an elephant in terms of its trunk, or in terms of its legs or in terms of its sides, or whatever bit of the elephant he happens to touch. In the same way, theoretical description of a psychological process may refer either to mechanistic characteristics of the process, or to mentalistic sensations associated with the process, or to physiological substrates. Psychological processes can be described in different ways using 'hypothetical constructs' of different ontological status. Physiological, mentalistic and mechanistic 'hypothetical constructs' each provide a different kind of theoretical description and each kind of theoretical description can be used to explain behaviour. Under certain circumstances, it is possible to identify one kind of theoretical description with another.

The concept of identification between 'hypothetical constructs' can be used in two ways when constructing a theory. The first and simplest way is to *define* two 'hypothetical constructs' as being identified. That is, a psychologist constructing a theory would postulate the existence of a pair of hypothetical constructs which have the property of identification, and would introduce them into the theory on the basis that they are identified. A second use concerns the relationship between hypothetical constructs whose existence has already been established. Evidence for the existence of a hypothetical construct comes from observables whose occurrence is consistent with that hypothetical construct's existence. If the observables which provide evidence for different kinds of hypothetical construct are correlated, then one might suspect that the two hypothetical constructs are identified. Such correlations, however, must be treated with caution. When two hypothetical constructs are identified, the presence of one must be associated with the other on a one-to-one basis, not on the basis of probabilistic association. So when two hypothetical constructs are identified the observables indicating the hypothetical constructs should be consistent with the hypothesis of a one-to-one association. Different kinds of hypothetical construct may be correlated without being identified. When two hypothetical constructs are identified, the occurrence of one must always be accompanied by the presence of the other and data must be consistent with this one-to-one relation.

In principle every mentalistic and mechanistic hypothetical construct can be identified with a physiological hypothetical construct. In practice it may be difficult to discover the properties of the physiological hypothetical constructs which are identified with those mentalistic and mechanistic hypothetical constructs. Nevertheless one can say that in principle there must be a physiological hypothetical construct which is identified with any mentalistic or mechanistic hypothetical construct. The reason for this is that – leaving aside supernatural explanations of thought – thoughts should not occur without there being some corresponding physiological change. Mechanistic hypothetical constructs are introduced on the basis that the nervous system models events in the world outside. There must therefore be some form of identity between the 'as if' mechanistic hypothetical constructs and the underlying physiological substrate. In practice it may be difficult to describe the underlying physiological structure of thoughts or mechanistic concepts, but the knowledge that it exists is important for theory construction.

For any physiological hypothetical construct there may be a mechanistic or mentalistic hypothetical construct which could be identified with it, but there may not. Although some physiological hypothetical constructs can be given a mentalistic or mechanistic representation, this is not necessarily the case. Some physiological events will not result in changes in thoughts and they may have no mechanistic form of representation. Thus mentalistic and mechanistic hypothetical constructs must in principle be identified with a physiological hypothetical construct; physiological hypothetical constructs may in principle be identified with mentalistic or mechanistic hypothetical constructs; and mentalistic and mechanistic hypothetical constructs may in principle be identified with each other. The 'in principle overlap' between events which can be represented physiologically, mentalistically, or mechanistically can be illustrated through a Venn diagram. (figure 4.1)

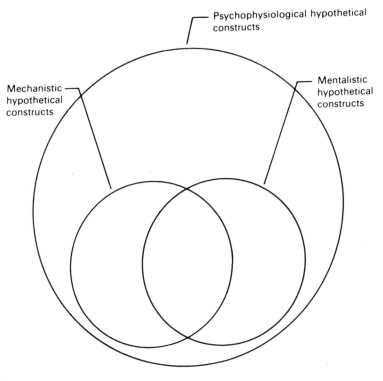

Figure 4.1

Identification is just one kind of relation that can occur between hypothetical constructs, and it is a relation which is based on the idea of separating hypothetical constructs into three different kinds. In the next chapter another sort of relation will be considered which also depends on a separation into three kinds of hypothetical construct: causal relations.

In this chapter the nature of theoretical concepts in psychology has been discussed. What has *not* been discussed is the nature of man. Questions relating to the nature of man fall within the province of philosophy, not within that of theoretical psychology. The aim of theoretical psychology is to provide useful explanations and that end can be achieved by using a variety of theoretical concepts. To a theoretical psychologist, the question is not 'Is man mechanistic' but 'Do mechanistic concepts provide a useful form of explanation'. Questions about whether man is an 'active' or 'passive' agent (a distinction which is not quite as clear as some would like to think) are outside the province of this book. Although mentalistic 'hypothetical constructs' may portray man as an 'active' agent, it does not necessarily have to be assumed that man is 'active' in order to adopt mentalistic 'hypothetical constructs' as a useful explanatory tool. In the same way, although mechanistic 'hypothetical constructs' may portray man as 'passive', mechanistic 'hypothetical constructs' may still provide a useful tool to explain the (or some) behaviour of an 'active' man. One purpose of theoretical psychology is to examine different kinds of explanation. The selection of a particular kind of explanation should be based ultimately, not on the philosophical question of the nature of man, but on the empirical question of the kind of explanation that provides the most useful and useable predictions.

5 Causal Relations in Psychology

The previous chapters have been concerned on the whole with the content or descriptive words of psychological theories. In these chapters a distinction was made between observable concepts such as the situation and behaviour and theoretical concepts which could either be intervening variables or 'hypothetical constructs'. Hypothetical constructs themselves are of three kinds, physiological, mentalistic and mechanistic. Hypothetical constructs of different kinds are sometimes identified. Identification is just one way in which descriptive concepts are related. In this chapter another sort of relation will be examined, causal relations.

The way in which different descriptive concepts are put together in a theory determines the *form* of a theory. The form of a theory consists of the kind of relationship which exists between the descriptive terms or content. In theoretical psychology, as in other scientific disciplines, causal relations play an important part in determining the form of a theory since descriptive words or content are often linked by words describing causal relations. In psychology, however, the concept of cause is far more complex than in other disciplines.

Psychologists often seem to find the word 'cause' a little embarrassing. Indeed there is good reason to be embarrassed, as the word cause is used to mean so many different things. One talks of physiological events causing physiological events; the mind causing physiological events (as in psychosomatic illness); mind states causing mind states; and in each case the concept of cause can be shown to have very different characteristics. Unfortunately, the use of a single word often obscures important conceptual differences, differences which must be specified if psychological causality is to be understood. This book suggests a convention for the use of the term 'cause' in psychology based on certain, easily applied criteria. (This convention,

incidentally, provides either a broader or a narrower definition of
the word cause than some other conventions.)

WHAT IS A CAUSE?

The word cause is used to represent a particular kind of relationship between occurrences or events. In everyday language, the
word cause is used both for occurrences with sequential relationships
and for occurrences with simultaneous relationships. For example,
one speaks of one billiard ball hitting another billiard ball and
causing it to roll away. The movement of the billiard balls is
sequential; one moves before the other. We also speak of 'the fact that
the electric fire is at $1000°$ C causes it to glow'. In the second example,
the two occurrences are different descriptions of the same event and
they occur simultaneously. There is no delay between the fire being at
$1000°$ C and its glowing. The concept of cause is thus commonly used
both for sequential and simultaneous relations. One constraint
placed here on the use of the word cause is that it should be applied
only to *sequential* relationships, that is, the word cause should only be
used for a relationship between events which occur at different times
or are temporally distinct (such a restriction is not uncommon, see,
for example, Hedman, 1972). The word cause should be restricted to
sequential events. Hence, in its simplest form 'cause' describes the
relationship between two events, the earlier or antecedent event is
referred to as the cause and the later or subsequent event is referred
to as the effect. When there are antecedent events and subsequent
events, then one refers to 'causes' and 'effects'.

The relationship described by the concept of cause enables
prediction: causes can be predicted from effects and effects from
causes. To put it the other way round, when it is possible to predict
from one event to another, when there is statistical regularity between
events, then (by definition) there must be some form of causal relation
which gives rise to this ability to predict, though the exact sort of
causal relation may not be clear. Correlation is an example where the
value of one variable can be predicted from another. If A and B are
truly correlated then *either* A causes B, *or* B causes A, *or* both A and B
are caused by C. There is no other possible explanation for a true
correlation between A and B: all explanations for the correlation
introduce the concept of cause. The way scientists perceive the
relationship between cause and prediction has changed over the

years. The initial approach was that causal relations enable one to provide deterministic predictions. The modern approach, stemming from nuclear physics, is that the prediction entailed in a causal relation may only be statistical. In this book the concept of cause will be used for predictive relationships which are either deterministic or statistical.

When one event causes another, some form of connection between the events is expected. One important characteristic of causal relations is that they conform to the principle of connectivity, that is, the events which are causally related should be connected in some way. In the billiard ball example, the balls are connected by means of spatial location: one ball hits or touches another. The feature of spatial connection is one of the characteristics of causality in the physical and natural sciences. In psychology, however, there are other kinds of connectivity as well. In psychology, there are different sorts of causal relation which are based on different kinds of connectivity.

So far some of the necessary conditions for the use of the word cause have been established. The word cause refers to a relationship between two or more temporally distinct events in which it is possible to predict one event from the other (statistical or deterministic) and in which the events have the characteristic of connectivity. In a theory the events comprise the content of the theory and the sort of causal connection depends on the nature of the content. Before examining the different sorts of causal connection that can occur in psychological theories, some of the different concepts which make up the content of a theory should be reviewed. The following list is based on distinctions made in previous chapters and provides sufficient information for distinguishing different sorts of causal relation.

Content of a Theory

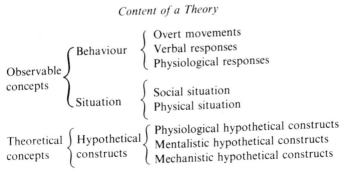

Causal relations between descriptive terms will be discussed under three headings: relations between hypothetical constructs; relations between hypothetical constructs and the situation; relations between hypothetical constructs and behaviour.

RELATIONS BETWEEN HYPOTHETICAL CONSTRUCTS

There is one very simple rule governing relationships between hypothetical constructs. Causal relations can exist between hypothetical constructs of the same ontological status, but they cannot exist between hypothetical constructs of differing ontological status. The reason for this rule is that connectivity occurs between the same kind of hypothetical constructs, but it does not occur between different kinds of hypothetical constructs.

Physiological hypothetical constructs are represented in space and exist in the same sense that physical objects exist. Causal relations between physiological hypothetical constructs can occur when there is some form of spatial connection between the hypothetical constructs. For example, a neurone might cause another neurone to fire because the two neurones are connected by a transmitter substance which is secreted by one of the neurones. The kind of causal relationship between physiological hypothetical constructs is the same as that between billiard balls. It is causality based on spatial connection. Causal relations between physiological hypothetical constructs therefore represent no novel problems as the relationship is the same as that found in other scientific disciplines.

Some authors have suggested that mind states cause mind states. Both Wundt's 'psychic causality' and William James' 'stream of consciousness' are based on the observation that mind states seem to follow a pattern and the idea of 'psychic causality' is introduced to account for this pattern. Mentalistic hypothetical constructs exist in the experience of the individual, they exist in the same sense that thoughts or experiences exist. Connections or 'associations' are found between different thoughts or experiences and it is these associations which form the basis of connectivity between mentalistic hypothetical constructs. Mentalistic hypothetical constructs are connected in experience. The kind of connectivity which relates mentalistic hypothetical constructs is different from the kind of connectivity which relates physiological hypothetical constructs; mental associations are different from spatial connectivity. So the concept of cause is being used in a different sense when it is used for relations between physiological hypothetical constructs than when it is used for relations between mentalistic hypothetical constructs.

Mechanistic hypothetical constructs exist in the sense of 'as if' mechanistic structures which have all the characteristics of those mechanistic structures. One of these characteristics is the property of causality. When causal relations between mechanistic hypothetical constructs occur, the mechanistic hypothetical constructs are connected by the spatial connection of the mechanistic structures with which they are described. Causal connection between mechanistic hypothetical structures is based on the spatial connection of the structures with which they are described. Mechanistic hypothetical constructs have a kind of 'as if' spatial connectivity, in contrast with the real spatial connectivity of the physiological hypothetical construct.

In summary, there are three forms of causality amongst hypothetical constructs; *physiological* causality between physiological hypothetical constructs, based on spatial connectivity; *mentalistic* causality amongst mentalistic hypothetical constructs, based on connectivity in experience; and *mechanistic* causality amongst mechanistic hypothetical constructs, based on 'as if' spatial connectivity. It is therefore possible to envisage causal relations between hypothetical constructs of the same ontological status though the kind of causality is different in each of the three cases. In only one of these cases, causality between physiological hypothetical constructs, is the word cause being used in the same sense as that found in the natural and physical sciences.

The next question to ask is whether it is possible for there to be causal relations between hypothetical constructs of differing ontological status. The answer to this question is clearly no. There is no kind of connectivity which would have the property of connecting differing kinds of hypothetical construct. Physiological hypothetical constructs cannot be causally linked to thoughts as one exists in space and the other exists in experience; similarly, neither of these can be linked to mechanistic hypothetical constructs which exist in a universe of 'as if' mechanistic structure. Causal relations between hypothetical constructs are therefore limited to relations between the same kind of hypothetical construct.

Causality is just one sort of relation that can occur between hypothetical constructs. Another sort of relation is identification; identification was described in the previous chapter. When the operational component of different kinds of 'hypothetical construct' are identical, then the 'hypothetical constructs' are said to be identified, or to have an identity relationship. Identity relations refer to occurrences which are simultaneous in time.

Identification between 'hypothetical constructs' provides a bridge which enables different kinds of process to be integrated. A process, it will be remembered, is a causal sequence which includes at least one hypothetical construct. As causal relations can only occur between hypothetical constructs of the same kind, there are therefore three different kinds of process. Physiological processes describe causal relations between physiological hypothetical constructs, mentalistic processes describe causal relations between mentalistic hypothetical constructs and mechanistic processes describe causal relations between mechanistic hypothetical constructs.

Processes describe events which are *sequential* in time. Imagine, for purposes of illustration, a series of events which could be described either physiologically, mentalistically, or mechanistically. That is, the events could (in principle) be described in terms of either a physiological, mentalistic or mechanistic process. This can be represented as follows

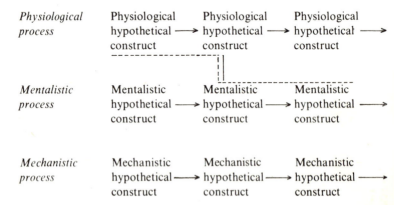

The arrows in the diagram represent causal connections. It can be seen that only hypothetical constructs of the same ontological status are causally connected. Movement in the horizontal direction on the

diagram is achieved through causal relations between hypothetical constructs. However, if two hypothetical constructs are identified, then it will also be possible to move vertically on the diagram. Suppose that a physiological hypothetical construct and a mentalistic hypothetical construct are identified, as indicated by the unbroken vertical line in the diagram. Identification between these two hypothetical constructs would provide a connection between the physiological process and the mentalistic process. For example, it would be possible to describe the earlier part of the causal sequence in terms of a physiological process and the latter part in terms of a mentalistic process. The identification between the mentalistic and physiological hypothetical construct acts as a bridge between the two kinds of process. This supposed integration between two kinds of process is indicated on the diagram by the path drawn out by the long, broken horizontal line. Thus, by using identity relations, two or more processes can be integrated into a single theory. A theory can consist of many integrated processes, where identification of hypothetical constructs provides a bridge between different kinds of process.

Why is it useful to be able to integrate different kinds of process? The reason is that it may not be possible to describe a sequence of events adequately in terms of only one kind of hypothetical construct. As will be seen in a moment, some observables, that is, some situations and behaviours, are more appropriately related to particular kinds of hypothetical construct. Depending on the sort of observables involved, it may be necessary to introduce more than one kind of process into a theory. The different processes are integrated through the use of identity relations.

In the diagram above one can see how it is possible to move between 'hypothetical constructs' in horizontal and vertical directions. Horizontal movement is achieved by causal relations, vertical movement by identity relations. It is not possible, however, to move in a diagonal direction. If one wishes to move to a 'hypothetical construct' which is in a diagonal position, then this must be achieved through a vertical and horizontal step (or a horizontal and vertical step). In writing a theory it is important to go through the full procedure of horizontal and vertical steps and not cut corners. If corners are cut, then the kinds of relation between concepts easily become ambiguous, and ambiguity in conceptual relationships is one of the weak points of current psychological theory.

RELATIONS BETWEEN HYPOTHETICAL CONSTRUCTS AND THE SITUATION

Hypothetical constructs are theoretical entities, they are unobservable. However, because they actually exist, they can be affected or modified by events which are observable. The situation can cause or have an effect on a hypothetical construct. Just as causality between hypothetical constructs must involve some form of connectivity between the hypothetical constructs, so too must causality between the situation and hypothetical constructs involve some form of connectivity. In practice this means that the situation must be expressed in a way which is consistent with the hypothetical constructs to which it is to be related.

The situation acts as a stimulus or 'input' to a process. Any one situation, however, can be described in a number of ways. Take, for example, the words 'I love you' which, spoken by one individual, act as a stimulus to some other individual. These words can be described as a particular pattern of vibrations in the air (for example, three separate clusters of vibrations) or they can be described in terms of the meaning embodied in the sentence (for example, sexual intent). When the situation is to be causally related to a hypothetical construct, the situation must be described in such a way that there is some form of connection between the stimulus and the hypothetical construct. The situation must be expressed in terms of the nature of the 'hypothetical construct' to which it is to be related. How is this done?

There are, as has been seen, three kinds of causality between hypothetical constructs; there are also three kinds of causality between situations and hypothetical constructs. The three kinds of causality between situations and hypothetical constructs are in fact the same as those between hypothetical constructs. For instance, if a stimulus is to be causally related to a physiological hypothetical construct, then the stimulus must have some physical characteristics which provide a connection with the physiological hypothetical construct. The physical characteristics of the situation must be described. Situations described as pinpricks or physical vibrations in the air both have the physical characteristic necessary to provide a causal connection with physiological hypothetical constructs, but the *meaning* of a pinprick ('I want to wake you up') or of the physical vibrations (sexual intent) do not. The meaning embodied in a situation does not have the necessary characteristics to provide a causal relation with a physiological hypothetical construct.

However, the meaning embodied in a situation is the aspect of the situation which is important when a situation is to be causally related to a mentalistic hypothetical construct. It is not the pinprick *per se* which affects the mentalistic hypothetical construct, rather it is what the pinprick means to the individual – how it is represented in his experience – which causes a change in the mentalistic hypothetical construct. To cause a mentalistic hypothetical construct, the situation must be described in terms of meaning.

Mechanistic hypothetical constructs exist in the sense of 'as if' mechanistic structures. If a situation is to be causally related to a mechanistic hypothetical construct, then the situation must be described in a way which is consistent with mechanistic structures. In other words, the situation must be described in the form of an input to some mechanistic system; in practice this means that the situation needs to be interpreted in a particular way so that it can be represented as the input to a mechanistic system. One of the advantages of mechanistic description is that many different aspects of the situation can be interpreted or 'reinterpreted' mechanistically. Physical aspects of a stimulus can easily be given a mechanistic interpretation (because they already have spatial characteristics), but more importantly the meaning embodied in a situation can also be given a mechanistic interpretation.

One of the characteristics of cognitive psychology is that meaning is interpreted mechanistically. Words in a memory task are represented as some kind of trace; the two sentences in a dichotic listening task might be referred to as two signals. Nevertheless, although it is very easy to find a mechanistic analogue of the meaning embodied in the situation, a mechanistic description of meaning can lead to problems. For example, consider the stimulus words 'I love you'. The meaning embodied in this statement can be represented as a particular kind of signal which inputs, say, to an 'affection component'. Suppose, to take the example further, that when the stimulus 'I love you' is repeated a number of times, this causes some change in the affection component which eventually leads to the mechanism (or person) responding in the form of an out-put 'I love you also'. The explanation provided in this example appears rather ridiculous because somehow one feels that the mechanistic description of complex human feelings is over-simplified; the mechanistic description does not really do justice to the meaning or nuances embodied in the sentence 'I love you'. It might be felt that love is more complex than a simple input to an affection component and so an explanation based on mechanistic description would be inadequate. When a mechanistic interpretation of the meaning embodied in a situation is given, some of the subtler shades of meaning which could be given in a mentalistic interpretation may be lost. The extent to which the description of the meaning is 'attenuated' by mechanistic interpretation depends on the particular meaning involved in the situation, but it cannot always be assumed that meaning can be adequately represented mechanistically. Although the meaning embodied in a situation can be given a mechanistic presentation, that representation may not always do full justice to the total meaning embodied in that situation.

In chapter 2, two broad categories of situations were distinguished: physical situations and social situations. In principle, any kind of situation can be causally related to any kind of hypothetical construct. In practice, however, certain sorts of situation can be related more conveniently or appropriately to particular kinds of hypothetical construct. For example, social situations are often best described in terms of the meanings of the actions of the participating individuals rather than in terms of their physical properties, and so social situations may more usefully be related to mentalistic or (depending on the kind of meaning) mechanistic hypothetical constructs. This does not mean, of course, that in explaining social behaviour one is committed to using mentalistic or mechanistic 'hypothetical constructs' throughout, only that in some circumstances it may be best to start the theory with a mentalistic or mechanistic construct. Some physical situations, on the other hand, may be better related to physiological hypothetical constructs, as it is the physical properties of the stimulus rather than the meaning which are important. When constructing a theory, one of the first things to decide is what kind of hypothetical construct should be used to form a causal relationship with the situation. The answer is provided, in part, by considering what aspects of the situation, that is what form of description, seems relevant to the explanation; one then chooses the kind of hypothetical construct which is consistent with this form of description. A particular selection is not right or wrong; it just results in one sort of 'attenuation of meaning' rather than another.

RELATIONS BETWEEN HYPOTHETICAL CONSTRUCTS AND BEHAVIOUR

Hypothetical constructs are theoretical entities and so unobservable. However, because they actually exist, they cause 'disturbances' or have consequences amongst events which can be observed. Hypothetical constructs can cause behaviour, that is, behaviour can be initiated or changed by hypothetical constructs. This causal relationship between hypothetical constructs and behaviour can be put to two uses.

First, the causal relationship between hypothetical constructs and behaviour can be used to explain the occurrence of that behaviour. When one wants to explain a particular behaviour it can be done in terms of some hypothetical constructs which give rise to that behaviour. Second, causal relations between hypothetical constructs and behaviour can be used to establish the validity of hypothetical constructs: information about a hypothetical construct can be gained because of its causal consequences on behaviour. These two uses are not mutually exclusive. Thus, in an explanation a hypothetical construct may be causally related to the *behaviour to be explained* and it may also be related to other *supplementary behaviours*.

Just as the situation and theoretical events may be described in different ways, so there are different ways of describing behaviour. When a hypothetical construct is to be causally related to behaviour, the behaviour must be described in a way which is consistent with the nature of the hypothetical construct. The behaviour must be described in such a way that there is a connection between it and the hypothetical construct. For behaviour to be causally related to a physiological hypothetical construct, the behaviour must be represented in a way which is consistent with physiological functioning, such as overt movements or physiological responses. Mentalistic hypothetical constructs, on the other hand, must be related to the meaning embodied in an action. For example, a physiological hypothetical construct might be causally related to arm movement, a mentalistic hypothetical construct to shaking hands. Mechanistic hypothetical constructs must be related to a mechanistic interpretation of the behaviour, and in practice this means representing the behaviour as the output to some mechanistic system.

When behaviour is described in the form of an output of some mechanistic system, it is possible to include in that description some of the meaning embodied in the behaviour. However, just as mechanistic interpretation of meaning in a situation may be inadequate, so may there also be some attenuation in meaning when the meaning embodied in a behaviour is described mechanistically.

In chapter 2, three ways of measuring behaviour or three sorts of behavioural data were given: overt movements, verbal statements and physiological responses. In principle, each kind of behaviour can be causally related to any kind of hypothetical construct. But, as with the situation, some sorts of behaviour are more conveniently related to particular kinds of hypothetical construct. For example, verbal statements are usually described in terms of the meaning embodied in the statement. The interest is usually not in the number of words a person says, but in what those words mean. So verbal statements are often more conveniently related to mentalistic or mechanistic hypothetical constructs. Physiological responses, on the other hand, may be more conveniently related to a physiological or mechanistic hypothetical construct. Movement could be related to any kind of hypothetical construct, depending on what aspect of the movement one wants to describe. For example, shaking hands should be related to a mentalistic or mechanistic hypothetical construct; repeated arm movement to a physiological or mechanistic hypothetical construct.

Particular kinds of behaviour can be more conveniently related to particular kinds of hypothetical construct. When constructing a theory, one has to decide on the particular kind of hypothetical construct which is to be causally related to the behaviour to be explained. Again, the selection will not be right or wrong: it just results in one sort of 'meaning attenuation' rather than another.

It may happen that the kind of hypothetical construct which is causally related to the situation may be different from that which is causally related to the behaviour. In such an instance, the two hypothetical constructs cannot have a causal relation with each other and so the theory must include two processes where the two processes are 'joined' by means of an identity relation between two hypothetical constructs. The identity relation 'joins' the two different kinds of process somewhere in the sequence of events between situation and behaviour.

Physiological Psychology and Psychophysiology

So far two different sorts of relation that can occur between the concepts which make up the content of a theory have been discussed identity relations and causal relations. The difference between these two sorts of relation is illustrated by the different aims of physiological psychology and psychophysiology. The aim of physiological psychology is to examine causal relations *either* between physiological hypothetical constructs, *or* between the situations and physiological hypothetical constructs, *or* between physiological hypothetical constructs and behaviour. These aims are usually achieved *either* by altering one part of the nervous system (for example, by stimulation or ablation) and then observing how this affects some other part of the nervous system; *or* by changing the situation and observing how this affects part of the nervous system (for example, Hubel and Wiesel's classic work on detectors in the brain); *or* by altering part of the nervous system and observing how these changes affect behaviour. These different techniques are all aimed at establishing causal relations.

The aims of psychophysiology are quite different from those of physiological psychology. Psychophysiology can have one of two aims. At an empirical level a researcher may be interested in finding the correlates of different measures of behaviour. For example he may measure EEG whilst the subject either engages or does not engage in eye contact or he may measure GSR in relation to verbal statements. Although correlations between physiological measures and other measures of behaviour can be treated atheoretically it is also possible to use such correlations for theoretical purposes, and this theoretical use constitutes the second aim of psychophysiology. Correlations between different measures of behaviour can be used as evidence that the hypothetical constructs which cause those behaviours may be identified. Thus, whereas physiological psychology is concerned with establishing causal relations, psychophysiology when interpreted theoretically can be used to establish identity relations.

Mentalistic hypothetical constructs, reasons and causes

Mentalistic hypothetical constructs include all the different and varied contents of consciousness. One sort of content of consciousness is the reason people give for their actions. Reasons can therefore feature as part of a causal explanation. Many philosophers, however, maintain that reasons are not causes (there are exceptions; see for example Davidson, 1963). Their argument goes as follows: reasons refer to *future* goals and are therefore located 'out of the world'; causes refer to *past* events and are therefore 'in the world'; hence reasons are not causes. There is, however, a difference in the way theoretical psychologists and philosophers use reasons to explain behaviour. Philosophers (and those psychologists adopting their tradition) explain behaviour by describing the reason one could have for engaging in that particular behaviour. Theoretical psychologists, on the other hand, explain behaviour by the fact that a person has a reason. The theoretical psychologist does not explain behaviour in terms of reasons, but by the fact that a person has a reason (for example Meehl, 1970; Lewin, 1943). When a person has a reason for carrying out an action, that reason exists as an experience prior to the occurrence of the action. Thus the fact that a person has a reason is not located 'out of the world' in some future state. Rather, it exists 'in the world' as an experience which occurs prior to the behaviour it causes. To the theoretical psychologist, reasons are just one sort of mentalistic hypothetical construct which can be used to predict the occurrence of behaviour. The reason explains behaviour by virtue of a statistical association between the kind of thought entailed in the reason, and the occurrence of a particular sort of behaviour. To the theoretical psychologist, reasons do not explain behaviour *except* by virtue of an observed thought–behaviour relationship. To a psychologist reasons need not be logical or even realistic; however, the subjects experience of a reason must predict a particular sort of behaviour. The philosopher's use of the term 'reason' must not be confused with that of the theoretical psychologist.

Causal processes and pseudoprocesses

The difference between causal processes and pseudoprocesses is a characteristic of science in general and not peculiar to psychology. A theory should enable one to anticipate and predict events, and it has this property because it describes causal relations. Causal relations obey laws; they are lawlike and so can be used for prediction. Earlier in this chapter certain necessary characteristics of causal relations were listed: they concern events which are temporally separate; they entail predictability which can either be deterministic or statistical; and they involve some form of connectiveness between causally related events. However, there are certain relations which satisfy the above conditions and yet which are not causal.

Imagine a revolving beacon which throws a moving spot of light onto a screen (figure 5.1). Every time the beacon revolves, the spot of

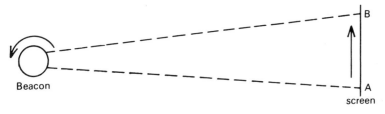

Figure 5.1

light moves across the screen. The movement of the spot of light conforms to the principles of prediction and connectivity. Once the spot is in position *A* we can predict that it will be soon in position *B*. At the same time, the spots at *A* and *B* are connected by the spatial location of the screen. However, although the moving spot of light fulfils the necessary criteria which must be satisfied for there to be causal relations, clearly the spot of light at point *A* does not cause the spot of light at point *B*. Instead, they are both the effects of a changing common cause: the revolving beacon. In the same way, the image of a man on the television screen who 'kicks the ball' is not causing the image of the ball to travel across the screen. Both the movement of the image of the man and the movement of the ball are caused by changing electrical fields. What are the differences between these non-causal relations which look deceptively like a causal relation and a true causal relation?

If a piece of coloured glass is placed in front of a beam of light, then the colour of the beam is changed – it has been *marked* (figure 5.2).

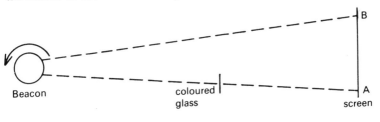

Figure 5.2

This mark will be found wherever the beam travels after it passes through the piece of coloured glass. It will be found at points far away from or near to the coloured glass and the transference of the mark occurs because the beam of light represents a true causal process. In our example of a revolving beacon, suppose we were to place a piece of coloured glass over point A on the screen. As the beacon shines onto point A the spot of light will be coloured, but the mark does not transfer when the spot moves to point B. The mark will only be local. The mark will not transfer to other places because the moving spot is a pseudoprocess rather than a causal process. Causal processes and pseudoprocesses can be distinguished by adding a mark and seeing whether the mark is transferred. In scientific methodology the experiment (discussed in chapter 9) provides a paradigm for deciding whether a relation is causal or not, and it does so in terms of manipulated or marked independent variables.

The difference between causal processes and pseudoprocesses stems from the relation between correlation and cause. When two events are correlated then one may be causing the other; or they may both result from a common cause. Whenever one observes or infers a sequence, whether the sequence is observable or theoretical, then that sequence may either be a causal process or a pseudoprocess. Just because a series of events follows a regular sequence, one cannot be certain that the relations between the events are causal. People tend to be rather bad at distinguishing causal processes from pseudoprocesses. Whenever a sequence of events follows a regular pattern then people will often assume that there are causal relations between the events (see Michotte's (1954) classic experiment) when in fact the sequence may be a pseudoprocess. Failure to distinguish between causal processes and pseudoprocesses can easily be a stumbling block in the construction of theories. A good example of such a failure can be found in some of the conceptualisations of psychosomatic disorders.

In psychosomatic illness particular sorts of thoughts, call them 'illness-orientated thoughts', are often followed by the onset of illness. Because illness often follows the illness-oriented thoughts, one can easily assume that there is a direct causal relation between the thoughts and the illness. For instance, one might even go so far as to suggest that the mind state is in some way causing the growth of bacteria. However, it is quite unnecessary to introduce these strange metaphysical notions of mind over matter when explaining psychosomatic illness if correct causal relations are observed. In psychosomatic illness the illness-orientated thoughts are identified with a particular physiological state. At the moment one may not be sure what the physiological state should be, but one can be certain that the illness-orientated thoughts are, like any other thought, identified with a particular physiological state. The physiological state causes other physiological changes such as hormone changes, which then act as a contributory cause to the onset of illness. The illness is psychosomatic simply because it is the thoughts (which are identified with the physiological state which causes the illness) that are noticed by the researcher. Psychosomatic illness can be explained in terms of two processes, a mentalistic process and a physiological process, which are joined through an identity relation between illness-orientated thoughts and a physiological state. The mentalistic process might explain the aetiology of illness-orientated thoughts, the physiological process might explain how a state identified with those thoughts contributes to the onset of illness. Thus, psychosomatic illness can be explained without any conceptual difficulty by using legitimate relations between concepts.

In this chapter causal relations between concepts in psychology have been examined. One assumption that has been made is that psychological phenomena are what can loosely be described as natural phenomena. The possibility of supernatural phenomena or supernatural relations has not been considered. If it were to be established that mind can directly and independently cause matter, or if there is the possibility of thought transference or whatever, then it will become necessary to introduce new sorts of causal relation into our theoretical framework. However, psychological opinion does not, at the moment, seem to require the introduction of these new forms of relationship.

6 Operators

What exactly is meant when one says that a hypothetical construct has a causal relation with another hypothetical construct, or that a hypothetical construct has a causal relation with the situation or behaviour? Any particular hypothetical construct, situation or behaviour can occur in different states; each of these concepts can vary. For example, the hypothetical construct 'memory store' might vary in terms of the content of memory; 'feeling depressed' might vary in terms of the intensity of this feeling. For any hypothetical construct, situation or behaviour, there will be variation sometimes along a single dimension (such as intensity), sometimes along a number of dimensions. Causal relations are concerned with the transition from one state to another; causal relations are concerned with the variation of a hypothetical construct along some dimension. What is meant by saying that hypothetical construct A causes hypothetical construct B is that the effect of A on B is such as to change B from one state to another. Causal relations are introduced to explain change: the 'effect' is changed by the 'cause'.

When A causes B, A causes a change in the state of B. This change is of a particular kind: A affects B in a particular manner. The particular kind of change is described by a function which is called an operator. An operator is a function which describes a kind of change. Before expanding on the concept of an operator, it should be mentioned that a 'kind of change' can be represented conceptually in more than one way. The way an operator is described here is not the only way of representing a 'kind of change', but it is for present purposes the most convenient.

Operators describe the form of the relationship between causally related events. An operator can be represented mathematically as a function which maps between the states of two events, that is, events which are causally related. An operator consists of the relationship between cause and effect. However, an operator can also be treated as an object. Imagine there is a set of operators which is related to

76

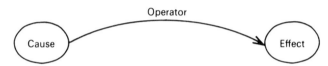

another set of operators, or with the same operators at a different point in time. The relationship between the two sets of operators can be described by another function, one which relates sets of objects called operators.

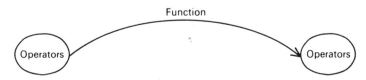

Thus operators can be described as the objects which make up a relationship, as well as being described as a relationship made up from some other objects. However, if operators are treated as objects, then they are a different *order* of object from the objects they relate when treated as a relationship. Mathematically (Ramsey, 1931, pp. 1–81) objects (zero-order objects) are distinguished from functions (first-order objects) which are distinguished from functionals (second-order objects). It is important that these different orders of objects are distinguished in psychological theories, although it should be noted that psychologists do not at the moment have a term for the psychological equivalent of a functional – that is, a function which relates operators.

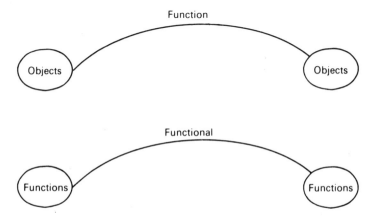

SIMPLE AND COMPLEX OPERATORS

It is possible to distinguish two sorts of operators: simple operators and complex operators. Simple operators will be dealt with first. Imagine two sets labelled hypothetical construct *A* and hypothetical construct *B*. The elements of the two sets are the states of hypothetical construct *A* and hypothetical construct *B*, and the simple operator is a function which maps between these two sets of elements. When hypothetical construct *A* is in one particular state, then this will cause hypothetical construct *B* to be in another particular state. The operator links all possible states of hypothetical construct *A* with those of hypothetical construct *B*. In other words, the operator tells us how hypothetical construct *A* affects hypothetical construct *B*. A simple operator, then, describes how a causal relationship is effected in terms of state-to-state linkages. It specifies what state an effect will be in for every state of the cause.

Complex operators are best explained by an example. Imagine two billiard balls: ball *A* and ball *B* (figure 6.1). Suppose that the two billiard balls represent different events and the position and movement of the balls represent states of those events. Ball *A* hits ball *B* and causes it to roll away. Evidently, the state of *A* at the moment of impact, its velocity and direction, determines the new position of *B*. The new position of *B* can be accurately predicted just from a knowledge of the state of *A* at or before the time of impact; in our example, the state of *A* causes the state of *B*.

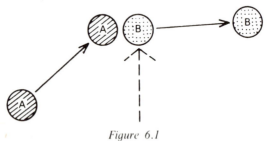

Figure 6.1

However, this simple rule only holds if *B* is stationary. If *B* is moving, then the end position of *B* depends not only on the state of *A* at the time of impact, but also on the state of *B* at the time of impact. Suppose that at the time of impact *B* is moving in the direction indicated by the dotted arrow; it will now end up in a very different position than if it were stationary. The simple case where an operator maps between states of *A* to states of *B* is a special limiting case where the initial state of *B* has no effect on the eventual outcome of the causal relation. Although some causal relations may be of this simple kind, there will also be instances where the effect of *A* on *B* depends also on the initial state of *B*. In the latter case of *complex operators* the operator specifies a function between the states of one event and transitions in the state of another event.

If two events *A* and *B* are causally related and that relationship takes the form of a complex operator, then the complex operator is a function which maps between states of *A* and transitions or changes in the state of *B*. The complex operator describes a relation between states of causes and transitions in the states of effects. The transitions in states of the effect can be described in terms of initial-state/end-state pairs. Each and every state of the cause is related to a series of initial-state/end-state pairs, initial-state/end-state pairs which result from all possible initial states of the effect.

In sum, operators may either be simple or complex: in the simple case when *A* causes *B* then the resulting state of *B* depends only on the state of *A*; in the complex case, the resulting state of *B* depends on the state of *A* and also on the initial state of *B*. Causal relations between two hypothetical constructs, or between the situation and a hypothetical construct, or between behaviour and a hypothetical construct can either take the form of a simple operator or of a complex operator.

The concept of a complex operator is not an easy one to grasp, so the point will be illustrated further with another example. Imagine a theory which describes the relation between new information and attitude change – in other words, between the situation 'communication' and a hypothetical construct 'attitude'. To be more specific, imagine a theory which describes the effect of hearing the statement 'chocolates are nice' on a person's attitude towards chocolates. The individual's attitude towards chocolates ought to change to a more positive state after hearing the 'chocolates are nice'. But it is evident that the individual's attitude after hearing the statement will depend not only on the statement, but also on his original liking for chocolates. If he began by detesting chocolates, then his attitude is going to end up being more negative than if he began by liking chocolates; so the effect of the situation on the hypothetical construct depends not only on the situation (the statement 'chocolates are nice') but also on the initial state of the hypothetical construct (his original attitude position towards chocolates). The resulting state of *B* depends not only on the state of *A*, but also on the initial state of *B*.

It is possible to imagine a number of ways in which the original attitude position can influence the eventual outcome. For example, the attitude statement may cause a constant change (linear transition) in attitude, the attitude changing a constant amount irrespective of the original position. Each time one hears that chocolates are nice, one's attitude might move another couple of points in a positive direction. Alternatively, the extent of change may not be constant (non-linear transition): the extent of change may depend on the size of the discrepancy between the new material and the original attitude position, or in other words on the relationship between the state of the statement and the state of the attitude. In fact experimental evidence (Whittaker, 1968) does suggest that extent of attitude change depends on the discrepancy between the original attitude position and the positivity of the communicated material. The relationship follows an inverted U-shaped curve: when the discrepancy between the new information and the attitude position is either very small or very large, then very little attitude change takes place; when the discrepancy falls between these two extremes, then the extent of attitude change is much greater. Thus the causal relation between attitude statements and attitude change is a complex operator which entails a non-linear transition.

Consequences of using simple and complex operators

Woodworth's S–O–R formulation carries the implication that the situation causes the organism which in turn causes behaviour. By placing the situation temporally antecedent to the organism one could infer that the state of the organism depends only on the situation. In other words one could infer from the S–O–R formulation that the situation and organism are related by means of a simple operator. If the situation and organism are related by a simple operator then the organism and hence behaviour will be determined by the situation. The assumption that behaviour is largely determined by the situation is a characteristic of behaviourist orientated or situationist approaches to psychology, approaches which in the past have been associated with the S–O–R formulation.

Lewin's $B = f(PE)$ formulation (behaviour is a function of the person and his environment) does not carry the implication that either the situation or individual are temporally antecedent. If the situation is related to a hypothetical construct by a complex operator then the initial state of the hypothetical construct will also determine behaviour. A complex operator is used when neither the situation nor the individual are the more important as determinants of behaviour.

A complex operator can also be used, however, when the individual is the more important determinant of behaviour. If the end-state of a hypothetical construct is largely determined by its initial state and the situation only affects the end-state slightly then behaviour will be largely under the control of individual characteristics. The emphasis on prior individual characteristics is a feature of psychoanalytic explanations. According to psychoanalytic tradition, the id does not change according to external stimuli, it bubbles away by itself! Thus, the choice of simple or complex operators relating the situation to a hypothetical construct does tend to produce different sorts of theory. The exclusive use of simple operators leads to theories which have been labelled situationist (Bowers, 1973) because of their emphasis on the situation as a determinant of behaviour. The use of complex operators can (but need not) lead to 'trait psychology', a psychology which places emphasis on the individual and very little on the situation.

Different sorts of operator should be used according to the kind of relationship one wishes to portray.

(1) When describing the relation between two hypothetical constructs, a simple operator describes a relation where the state of the causing hypothetical construct alone determines the state of the caused hypothetical construct; a complex operator describes a relation where the final state of the caused hypothetical construct also depends on its initial state.

(2) When describing the relation between the situation and a hypothetical construct, a simple operator describes a relation where the state of the hypothetical construct is determined solely by the state of the situation; a complex operator describes a relation where the state of the hypothetical construct is also determined by the hypothetical construct's prior state.

(3) When describing the relation between a hypothetical construct and behaviour, a simple operator will describe a relation in which the caused behaviour is determined solely by the state of the causing

hypothetical construct; a complex operator will describe a relation where the caused behaviour is dependent on prior behaviour.

DIFFERENCES IN THE FORM OF AN OPERATOR

The form of any particular operator may vary; that is, the particular associations between states and states (as in the case of a simple operator) or between states and transitions in states (as in the case of a complex operator) may vary. The idea of variation or change in the form of an operator is independent of whether it is simple or complex. For example, operator X which is simple may change its form and remain simple or it may change its form and become complex; similarly operator Y which is complex may change its form and remain complex or become simple. To illustrate what is meant by change in the form of an operator, the example of information and attitude change will serve again. Information and attitude change are related by a complex operator and the relation takes the form of an inverted U-shaped curve. In this relationship the shape of the U may vary – it could become flattened, or it could become skewed one way or the other – and such variation constitutes change in the form of the operator relating information and attitude. The possibility of an operator having different forms is important for two reasons: first, it provides a means for describing individual differences, that is, differences in behaviour between different individuals. Second, it provides a means for describing individual change, that is, differences over time within the same individual. Individual differences and individual change occur for the same reasons (they just involve different objects of comparison) and so they can be considered together.

Individual differences or individual change can occur for one of two reasons: *either* because hypothetical constructs are in different states, *or* because operators have different forms. Theories accounting for individual differences or individual change can involve either kind of difference.

The simplest way of describing individual differences or individual change is to posit that differences occur because hypothetical constructs are in different states. Suppose that a group of students is presented with a list of nonsense syllables. Some students can remember the list and some cannot. The difference between these two groups of students can be attributed to the fact that hypothetical construct 'memory store' is in a different state for each group. The 'memory store' for students remembering the list contains 'traces' of the nonsense syllables whereas the 'memory store' of those forgetting the list does not. Over time the students who remembered the list will gradually forget it and this forgetting can be attributed to the fact that for each individual, the hypothetical construct of 'memory store' is in different states at different times – the 'traces' gradually disappear. Thus, one way of accounting for individual differences or change is to describe differences in the state of a hypothetical construct. Evidently, the kind of difference which can be described in this way will be rather specific as it will refer only to the states of one hypothetical construct.

A second way of accounting for individual differences or individual change is to describe differences in the form of an operator. Imagine how one might represent the individual difference 'state anxiety'. (Level of state anxiety is specific to particular situations. State anxiety is distinguished from trait anxiety which does not vary with situations.) State anxiety can be represented as an operator relating the situation to the mentalistic hypothetical construct of 'feeling worried' – a hypothetical construct which varies in intensity. One of the characteristics of state anxiety is that certain situations cause high levels of feeling worried. In the case of state anxiety there is not a general tendency to be worried irrespective of the situation, rather *specific* situations lead to the sensation of worry. The difference between people high in state anxiety and those low in state anxiety is described by differences in the form of the operator which relates situations to the sensation of feeling worried (the hypothetical construct). Low state anxiety individuals hardly feel worried (or no more worried than is reasonable) whatever the situation; high state anxiety individuals feel extremely worried in certain specific situations. One individual may feel worried in the presence of dogs, but quite unconcerned in open spaces. Another may be unworried by dogs, but considerably worried by open spaces. Individual differences in state anxiety, then, can be described as differences in the form of the operator relating situations to intensity of the sensation of feeling worried.

If trait or free-floating anxiety were to be described, then it could easily be represented as variation in the state of a hypothetical construct. High anxiety individuals tend to be generally more worried than low anxiety individuals, so that in the high anxiety individual the hypothetical construct feeling worried would be in a different state (that is, more intense) from that of the low anxiety individual. However, because it is situation specific, state anxiety cannot be represented as variation in the state of a hypothetical construct. Or can it? Consider how it might be possible to represent state anxiety as variation in the state of the hypothetical construct. Instead of having a hypothetical construct feeling worried which varies only in one dimension of intensity, suppose that the hypothetical construct feeling worried is represented as varying in a number of different dimensions. For instance, one dimension could consist of intensity in feeling worried about dogs, another intensity about feeling worried about open spaces. Many more dimensions would have to be added, such as worry about spiders, snakes and so on. It would now be possible to represent state anxiety as variation in the state of the hypothetical construct feeling worried along one of these many different dimensions. Hence, state anxiety can be represented as variation in the states of a hypothetical construct.

There are two problems with representing state anxiety in this way. One problem is that an uncomfortably large number of dimensions may be needed to represent state anxiety. A second problem is that it is always possible to come across a state specific anxiety which had not been heard of before. For example, an individual who is afraid of black boots may turn up, and so the individual difference of state anxiety may have to be redefined to include the dimension 'worry about black boots'. The point is that it is usually possible to represent an individual difference or change *either* as differences in the state of a hypothetical construct *or* as differences in the form of an operator. However, it is usually more convenient to represent difference or change one way rather than another, and it is this convenience which normally dictates choice. If one is just interested in describing an individual difference or individual change, then it may not make much difference whether one uses variation in the state of a hypothetical construct or variation in the form of an operator. Theoretical formulation has a certain flexibility in the way individual difference or change are represented. However, once individual differences or changes are introduced into a more general theory which achieves a degree of integration between different areas, then it can be quite important whether one uses differences in the state of a hypothetical construct or form of an operator. One conceptualisation may enable development of a much better theory than the other. So from the point of view of using individual differences or change in theory construction (and also to eliminate ambiguity) it is a good idea to make a point of specifying how these differences or change are represented.

IDENTITY RELATIONS BETWEEN OPERATORS AND HYPOTHETICAL CONSTRUCTS

Operators describe the relationship between the states of a cause and the states or transitions of states of an effect. Although operators *describe* the relationship between two causally related events, they do not *explain* that relationship. In chapter 1 it was remarked that the difference between a description and an explanation is that the explanation provides a description of events at a level other than that of the events being explained. Relations between observables can be *described* simply by providing a descriptive account of those observables, but in order to explain those relations an additional descriptive account is needed, normally at a theoretical level. When explaining observables, the observables are at a descriptive level, the theoretical terms are at an explanatory level. Operators, however, describe a relationship between concepts which are themselves at a theoretical level – at least one concept in the relation described by an operator is at a theoretical level. An operator must, therefore, be explained by referring to some other level of description which can act at an explanatory level. Fortunately, there are different kinds of theoretical description in psychology – physiological, mentalistic, and mechanistic – and it is these differences in theoretical description which form the basis for explaining operators.

An operator describes a causal relationship which will necessarily involve only one kind of hypothetical construct. That relationship can be explained by *identifying the operator with another kind of hypothetical construct*. It should be recalled that operators can be treated either as relationships or as objects. To explain the relationship entailed in an operator, the operator is treated as an object, an object which is identified with a hypothetical construct. The important point to note is that the nature of the hypothetical constructs entailed in the 'operator described as a relationship' is different from the nature of the hypothetical construct which is identified with the 'operator described as an object'. Thus, when an operator is identified with a hypothetical construct the hypothetical construct has a different nature to that entailed in the relationship described by the operator. The identified hypothetical construct provides an additional level of description, an additional level which acts to explain the relationship of the operator. The hypothetical construct which is identified with an operator provides additional information, information which is associated with that hypothetical construct's nature. In sum an operator can be described at a descriptive level – the level of the hypothetical construct(s) whose states are related – and can also be described at an explanatory level – some other theoretical level involving another kind of hypothetical construct. There are three kinds of hypothetical construct, so for any operator which relates one kind of hypothetical construct there are two other kinds of hypothetical construct which could explain that operator. Given a particular descriptive level there is an option between two other levels for use as an explanatory level.

What is the criterion for identity relations between operators and hypothetical constructs? An operator and a hypothetical construct are identified when changes in the form of the operator and changes in the state of the hypothetical construct lead to the same changes in behaviour. Identification between an operator and a hypothetical construct is defined by postulating that some change in the form of the operator and in the state of the hypothetical construct will lead to an identical difference or change in behaviour. Identification between operators and hypothetical constructs is thus defined in terms of covariation.

What is the advantage of providing an explanation for an operator? After all, when a hypothetical construct is identified with an operator, the hypothetical construct does not provide any new information about the form of the relationship between the concepts at the descriptive level. If the hypothetical construct at the explanatory level does not say anything new about the state to state or state to transitions in state links, why bother with the rather complicated idea of identification between operators and hypothetical constructs? The advantage of explaining an operator lies in the fact that the explanatory level provides additional means for predicting change in the form of the operator. If the form of an operator can vary, then an identified hypothetical construct enables description of additional parameters (associated with the hypothetical construct's nature) which predict changes in form. The advantage of an explanatory level is that it helps predict variation in the form of an operator.

So far the identification between an operator and a hypothetical construct has been discussed in a rather abstract way, and so to see how the explanatory and descriptive levels of an operator fit together an example modified from the experimental literature will be considered. Suppose that a person (Mr R) is placed at the beginning of a T-maze. When he reaches the junction he can turn either right or left. If he turns left and walks down the left-hand turning, Mr R, who is rather short-sighted, suddenly receives an electric shock. If he turns right, he suddenly comes across an enormous nipple protruding from the wall from which he can suck a sweet sticky liquid. Over time, Mr R learns to turn right rather than left. His behaviour can be explained in terms of a mentalistic hypothetical construct 'feeling afraid' which has two states, high fear and low fear. When Mr R reaches the junction of the T-maze the left-hand turning causes a change in the state of a mentalistic hypothetical construct feeling afraid causing Mr R to be in the state of high fear. The right-hand turning, however, causes the hypothetical construct feeling afraid to be in the state of low fear. Mr R only proceeds in a direction associated with the sensation of low fear and so he only proceeds down the right-hand arm of the T-maze. Diagrammatically, we can represent the explanation of Mr R's behaviour thus

Situation	Hypothetical construct	Behaviour
Left-hand turning $\longrightarrow$	Feeling afraid (state: high fear) $\longrightarrow$	Avoid
Right-hand turning $\longrightarrow$	Feeling afraid (state: low fear) $\longrightarrow$	Approach

In the diagram the arrows represent operators, other concepts are as labelled.

Now suppose that Mr R is injected with barbiturate and again trained in the T-maze, only this time the electric shock is located in the right-hand arm of the maze and the nipple is located in the left-hand arm. Over time, Mr R will learn these new positions, so that the left-hand arm leads to low fear, and the right-hand arm leads to high fear. One is now in a position to demonstrate a state-dependent learning effect: in the absence of barbiturate Mr R turns right, with barbiturate he turns left.

Explanations for Mr R's state-dependent behaviour can be represented thus

NO BARBITURATE

Situation	*Hypothetical construct*	*Behaviour*
Left-hand turning	→Feeling afraid (state: high fear) →	Avoid
Right-hand turning	→Feeling afraid (state: low fear) →	Approach

BARBITURATE

Left-hand turning	→Feeling afraid (state: low fear) →	Approach
Right-hand turning	→Feeling afraid (state: high fear) →	Avoid

Notice that the difference between the explanations in the barbiturate and non-barbiturate conditions lies in the *form* of the explanations. The *content* of the two explanations are identical. The difference between the two explanations lies in the form of the operator which relates the situation of left/right-hand turn to the hypothetical construct feeling afraid. In the barbiturate and non-barbiturate conditions, the relationship is reversed. How can this change be explained in the form of the operator between the two conditions? Suppose that barbiturate causes a physiological change. The precise nature of the change is not known but say that barbiturates change the state of physiological hypothetical construct X, which is defined as being identified with the operator relating the situation to the mentalistic hypothetical construct feeling afraid. Then changes in the state of the operator relating the situation to feeling afraid can be predicted from a knowledge of the state of hypothetical construct X. Information about the state of hypothetical construct X can be gained through its causal relation with barbiturates. So barbiturates constitute a parameter which can be used to predict change in the form of the operator. The operator involves a mentalistic hypothetical construct; barbiturates are physical entities. But barbiturates do not cause high fear or low fear. Barbiturates have a causal relation with a physiological hypothetical construct which in turn has an identity relation with an operator which in turn describes the causal relation between the situation and a mentalistic hypothetical construct.

Consider a second example. Suppose that one is in the habit of waking up (waking behaviour) when the cock crows – which it does regularly at 7 am. This waking behaviour can be explained in physiological terms: the cock crowing activates the reticular formation of the brain which then causes activation of the cortex and hence waking.

Cock crowing → reticular formation (active) → cortex → waking behaviour

Suppose that on Sundays one does not have to get up early in the morning. The cock crows at its usual time, but one does not wake up. This is because the cock crowing now no longer has the property of activating the reticular formation.

Situation	*Hypothetical construct*	*Behaviour*

WEEK DAYS
Cock crowing → Reticular formation (active) → Waking behaviour

SUNDAYS
Cock crowing → Reticular formation (not active) → Sleeping behaviour

The reason that the cock crow does not activate the reticular formation on Sundays is that one tells oneself on the Saturday night 'I don't have to get up to work tomorrow'. This instruction is represented mentalistically as a mentalistic hypothetical construct 'getting up intention' which has states yes and no. The mentalistic hypothetical construct is identified with the operator, which relates the situation to a physiological hypothetical construct. The mentalistic hypothetical construct does not cause changes amongst physiological events. Rather, changes in the state of the mentalistic hypothetical construct are the same as changes in the form of the operator relating the situation to the physiological hypothetical construct.

In both examples, changes in the form of an operator and changes in the state of a hypothetical construct lead to exactly the same change in behaviour, and it is because of this covariation that the operator and hypothetical construct are said to be identified. Notice that the identified hypothetical construct provides no more information about relations described by the operator, it merely enables one to predict when the form of the operator will change. The explanatory level, the identified hypothetical construct, helps in the prediction of change in the form of an operator. However, the explanatory level does not enable prediction of *all* forms of variation, it only enables prediction of a specific form of variation. The identified hypothetical construct can only predict that variation in the form of the operator which covaries with changes in the state of the hypothetical construct. The operator may vary in other ways, but it is only the covariation which can be explained by the identified hypothetical construct. In conclusion, when a hypothetical construct is identified with an operator, the hypothetical construct provides a means for predicting change in the form of the operator, but it only enables one to predict a specific sort of change.

At the moment, the concept of an operator is hardly used in psychology and this is despite the fact that it is relevant to all theoretical formulation. Concepts and relations between concepts (zero and first-order objects) are easily confused when constructing a theory. The possibility of such confusion is removed when a proper distinction is made between operators and the concepts they relate. Furthermore, when an operator is identified with a hypothetical construct it provides another technique for integrating different kinds of hypothetical construct into a single more comprehensive explanation. The idea of an operator has therefore considerable potential as a concept in theory construction and it should certainly play a larger part in the more sophisticated theories of the future.

7 Theories

Concepts in psychology can be related to each other in different ways. In this chapter these different relations will be drawn together and a theory considered as a whole. One of the most convenient ways of summarising a theory is to represent it diagrammatically. In this manner, each individual theory or diagram can be seen to be part of a more general theoretical framework or diagrammatic structure which encapsulates all the different possible kinds of theory which could be devised. Summaries of individual theories will be discussed by means of this general theoretical framework, since it provides a way of summarising theories in a consistent, diagrammatic form. Different theories can be compared and it is a useful conceptual tool in that it can act as a guide in theory formulation.

GENERAL THEORETICAL FRAMEWORK

Psychological theories entail a sequence of events or descriptions in time. The duration of the events described by the theory may be very short, almost instantaneous, or it may be very long, but in all cases a theory describes, amongst other things, events which are temporally distinct. When representing a theory in the form of a diagram the horizontal will be used as a time base: descriptions to the left of the page are antecedent to those on the right. The time base will only be used to achieve a qualitative temporal separation (that is, it serves as an ordinal scale rather than as a quantitative one).

The horizontal in theoretical diagrams depicts the time base. The vertical is divided into three sections, each depicting a different level of events (figure 7.1).

One section positioned at the top of the diagram refers to the situation; a second section positioned in the middle part of the diagram refers to behaviour; and a third section positioned at the bottom of the diagram refers to theoretical events. The three sections

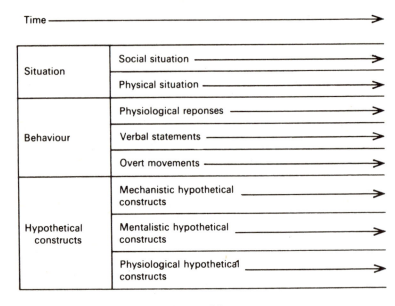

Figure 7.1

are themselves subdivided: the situation is subdivided into two categories, the social situation and the physical situation; behaviour is subdivided into three categories, physiological responses, verbal statements and overt movements; hypothetical constructs are subdivided into three categories, physiological, mentalistic, and mechanistic hypothetical constructs. Naturally further divisions could be made within each of these subdivisions. Each theory consists of a varying number of concepts which are located in each of the three sections; there must be at least one concept in each section, but more than one concept can appear within a single category. When concepts refer to descriptions which are simultaneous (that is, occur at the same time) they should be placed in a vertical line; when they refer to events which are not simultaneous they should be placed at different points along the horizontal axis.

Concepts can be related in the following ways.

(1) A *causal* relation is indicated by an arrow which connects the cause to the effect. Arrows are only used to denote causal relations and just one kind of arrow is used to indicate the different kinds of causality which can exist between concepts. Arrows should not be

placed in a vertical direction because causal relations do not occur between simultaneous occurrences. Since the form of a causal relation is described by an operator, the arrow itself represents an operator.

(2) An *identity* relation between hypothetical constructs should be indicated by an unbroken line between the identified hypothetical constructs. Identified hypothetical constructs are simultaneous occurrences and so the unbroken line should be placed vertically.

(3) An *identity* relation between an operator and a hypothetical construct should be indicated by an unbroken line joining the arrow representing the operator to the hypothetical construct. The unbroken line should be placed vertically.

When a theory is represented diagrammatically there will be a number of concepts located in each of the three sections, which are connected by lines and arrows. Naturally, the concepts and the ways they are connected are very diverse and so there is an almost infinite number of possible theories. Let us consider two examples of theories to see how summaries can be made within the general theoretical framework.

Example 1. Theory to explain change in level of performance in crowded situations (figure 7.2)

A crowded room causes an increase in the level of the mentalistic hypothetical construct 'perceived overcrowding'. 'Perceived overcrowding' causes the mentalistic hypothetical construct 'feeling aroused'. 'Feeling aroused' is identified with (*a*) a physiological hypothetical construct 'arousal' which causes a measurable physiological response (supplementary behaviour) and (*b*) a mechanistic hypothetical construct 'arousal'. The mechanistic hypothetical construct arousal causes a change in the state of the mechanistic hypothetical construct 'available capacity' which causes a change in the level of performance, the behaviour to be explained.

Example 2. Theory to explain approach/avoidance behaviour with state-dependent learning (figure 7.3)

This is the example from our last chapter of a theory to explain the behaviour of man in a T-maze. The physical situation of the junction of the T-maze causes the mentalistic hypothetical construct 'feeling afraid'. 'Feeling afraid' causes the behaviour approach/avoid, the

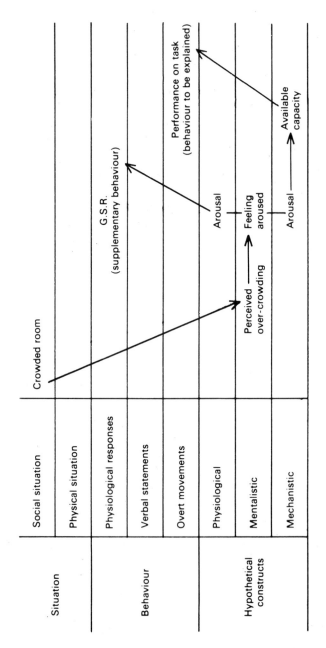

Figure 7.2 Theory: example 1

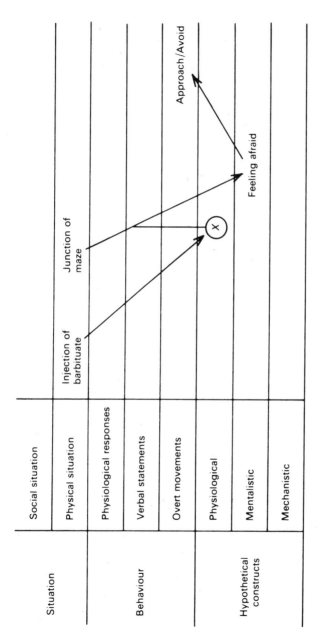

Figure 7.3 Theory: example 2

behaviour to be explained. The operator relating the physical situation to the mentalistic hypothetical construct 'feeling afraid' is identified with the physiological hypothetical construct X which is caused to vary by barbiturates.

These two examples of theories describe events occurring over a relatively short period of time and they entail a relatively small number of concepts. More elaborate theories can be built up from the same sort of concepts and relations between concepts. A more elaborate theory might, for example, introduce a number of situational factors which have causal relations with hypothetical constructs at different stages in the sequence. Alternatively, a single hypothetical construct or behaviour may be affected by a number of causes or a hypothetical construct or situation may cause a number of effects. Such cases of multicausality should be represented by a

A

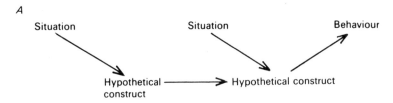

B

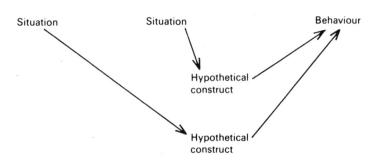

Figure 7.4 Examples of multicausality

number of arrows leading to or from the 'hypothetical construct', situation or behaviour (figure 7.4).

It is also possible that a behaviour may constitute a change in the situation, a change which acts as a stimulus for some later part of the sequence. The possibility that behaviour may also act as the situation gives rise to the idea of a 'feedback loop' between behaviour and the situation. This idea can be a bit misleading as it tends to detract from the temporal sequencing of a process, the fact that events are temporally distinct (see Kantor, 1969, p. 376). A 'feedback loop' between the situation and behaviour might be represented thus

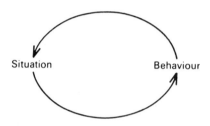

However, the relation between behaviour and the situation can be more correctly represented as

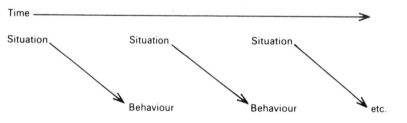

The situation causes the behaviour but the behaviour constitutes a new situation. The behaviour does not cause a new situation, it *is* a new situation. Thus, a 'feedback loop' between the situation and behaviour can be more correctly represented through the general theoretical framework where the pattern of reiteration is stretched out along a time base. Such reiterative patterns can occur not only between the situation and behaviour but also between any other concepts. However, in all cases, the 'feedback loop' is made more explicit by representing it as a reiterative sequence along a time base.

Diagrammatic representation through the general theoretical framework is a way of *summarising* theories and in so doing it provides a means for the easy comparison of theories. However, there is more to a theory than just its summary and along with diagrammatic representation a theory should also be described in detail using the kind of verbal description which has been examined in earlier chapters.

It follows from the above description that psychological theories vary in complexity. A very simple theory will consist of only one process which may include just one or two hypothetical constructs. A slightly more sophisticated theory will entail one process but will incorporate a number of hypothetical constructs. Complex theories will include a number of processes which are interrelated by means of identity relations and will include a number of different kinds of hypothetical construct.

Turning to theories as they actually occur in the literature, they tend to be very simple. Although cognitive psychologists often propose theories which involve a number of (mechanistic) hypothetical constructs one seldom finds a theory which involves more than one process. Indeed, in social psychology there are a number of single hypothetical construct theories – theories which could perhaps be criticised on the grounds that they constitute explanatory fictions (chapter 1). It seems to be the case that psychologists do not sufficiently exploit the theoretical facilities which are available. More use could be made of interrelations between different kinds of process, either through identification of hypothetical constructs or through identification between an operator and a hypothetical construct. More use could be made of multicausal relations between concepts and reiterative sequences.

Some psychologists, particularly those with phenomenological leanings, may feel that the kind of theory with which they are interested cannot be reduced to a mere diagram of interrelated concepts. The argument against such a view is that diagrammatic representation provides a summary of a theory, it does not provide a total description. However, any theory should be able to be summarised and hence represented diagrammatically and if it cannot it is because it has not been sufficiently thought out. Although the theory may have some useful features – it may, like Freud's theories, stimulate the developement of a therapeutic technique – it will not be high in predictive power. If a theory is insufficiently precise for diagrammatic representation, then it will not provide sufficient information to predict and control events; and it is these features of prediction and control which are the reasons for adopting theories in the first instance. By representing a theory in the form of a diagram one at least ensures that the general format of the theory is represented clearly and unambiguously. Note, however, that only a general account of the theory can be portrayed diagrammatically. Specific information about the content or the form of a theory must be provided separately. For example, it may be necessary to give a more precise rendering of the form of a theory through the use of mathematical description. Similarly, an exact characterisation of a hypothetical construct may require a descriptive paragraph or two. To repeat once again, diagrammatic representation provides a summary of a theory, it does not provide a complete description.

8 Explaining What?

The discipline of psychology is obviously divided into different areas of study. There are three different ways or criteria which are used to separate these different areas, on the basis: (*a*) the kind of explanation provided; (*b*) the characteristics of the behaviour which is to be explained; and (*c*) the characteristics of the situation in which the behaviour to be explained occurs. The first criterion, the kind of explanation provided, is one which has been of concern in previous chapters. It has been shown that processes can incorporate either physiological, mentalistic or mechanistic hypothetical constructs. The use of any of these three kinds of hypothetical construct divides psychology into different areas which can be called *kinds* of psychology. Physiological psychology and psychophysiology are associated with the use of physiological hypothetical constructs; phenomenological, or existential and humanistic psychology are associated with the use of mentalistic hypothetical constructs; cognitive psychology is associated with the use of mechanistic (or sometimes mentalistic) hypothetical constructs. One argument pursued in this book is that the different kinds of explanations in psychology need not be completely separated, and that explanations drawing on different kinds of psychology are possible.

The second criterion for separating areas of study – characteristics of the behaviour which is to be explained – divides psychology into areas which will be called *topics*, and it is these which will be examined, albeit at an elementary level, in this chapter. The third criterion for dividing psychology into areas, the characteristics of the situation in which the behaviour to be explained occurs, is not important from the point of view of theoretical psychology and will be mentioned only briefly at the end of the chapter.

In chapter 4 it was remarked that one of the functions of a hypothetical construct is to explain behaviour. Behaviour, however, has many characteristics and different sorts of concept must be used to explain these different characteristics. Consider first what is meant by a characteristic of behaviour. If one looks at different behaviours, it appears that certain features seem to occur regularly. For example, many behaviours are goal-orientated. Sometimes different people will behave differently in different situations. Sometimes a person's behaviour is permanently affected by interaction with a situation. These regularly occurring features are characteristics of behaviour. Psychologists introduce what will be called *explanatory concepts* to explain these characteristics of behaviour. Explanatory concepts are described by their function: they have the function of explaining a particular characteristic of behaviour. It is these explanatory concepts such as learning, motivation, perception, personality, and performance which form the basis for dividing psychology up into topics.

Psychology is divided into topics on the basis of characteristics of behaviour to be explained. However, one thing that makes the issue of explanatory concepts rather complex is that the characteristics of behaviour which divide psychology into topics are not mutually exclusive. A particular behaviour may have many characteristics. So, not only must explanatory concepts themselves be examined, but also one must consider combined explanatory concepts such as motivated perception or performance in learning.

Explanatory concepts are represented theoretically through the use of 'hypothetical constructs' and they can be represented in one of two ways. *Either* they can refer to a hypothetical construct or a group of hypothetical constructs which explain the behavioural characteristic specified by the explanatory concept; *or* they can refer to a difference or change or relation between hypothetical constructs which explain the behavioural characteristic specified by the explanatory concept. In this chapter explanatory concepts which refer to hypothetical constructs are examined first and then explanatory concepts which refer to differences, changes or relations between hypothetical constructs.

EXPLANATORY CONCEPTS WHICH REFER TO HYPOTHETICAL CONSTRUCTS

Explanatory concepts which refer to hypothetical constructs can be divided into three categories: energy concepts, directional concepts and performance concepts. Energy concepts and directional concepts make up a topic in psychology called motivation. Motivation is concerned with the explanation of goal-orientated behaviour. Energy and directional concepts explain the characteristic of goal-orientatedness of behaviour. Peters (1958) was one of the first to observe that the study of motivation is concerned with two sorts of concept, drives and motives as he called them. A similar two-component system was arrived at independently by Davidson, 1963. Peters' distinction of drives and motives is similar to the distinction being used here of energy and directional concepts, though, unlike Peters, the term motivation is used to cover both sorts of concept.

An energy concept is similar to the traditional concept of drive. It describes the energy, force or drive which induces people to engage in goal-orientated behaviour. It explains variation in the intensity of goal-orientated behaviour, doing so in terms of variation in the amount of energy or level of drive. An energy concept refers to a hypothetical construct which motivates people to engage in goal-orientated behaviour and variation in intensity of goal-seeking behaviour is described by variation in the state of the hypothetical construct. A directional concept, on the other hand, explains why a drive is satisfied in one way rather than another. It explains the direction of goal-orientated behaviour or choice that people adopt to achieve the goals specified in the energy component. A directional concept refers to a hypothetical construct where differences in the state of the hypothetical construct indicate different directions or choices. Energy concepts explain the *intensity* of goal-orientated behaviour; directional concepts explain *directionality* of goal-orientated behaviour.

Energy concepts

Psychologists often suggest that there is an energy, force or drive which motivates people to attain certain sorts of goal, objective or end-state. A hypothetical construct can be postulated which has the property of motivating people to attain these end-states or goals, and the end-states or goals are specified in the description of the hypothetical construct. Energy concepts can refer to any kind (physiological, mentalistic or mechanistic) of hypothetical construct and depending on the kind of hypothetical construct used, the end-state will be expressed either physiologically, mentalistically, or mechanistically. For example, when one says that people are motivated to avoid the physiological state of hunger, hunger drive can be represented physiologically as variation in activity of part of the hypothalamus. Again, some people are motivated to attain the goal of salvation and salvation can be represented mentalistically. Here the motive towards salvation is a *feeling* that salvation is a good thing to have. As an example of mechanistic representation, the motive 'need for achievement' can explain behaviour directed towards the attainment of financial gain. 'N-Ach' can be represented as a mechanistic component leading to a particular 'high output' of achievement-orientated behaviour.

Thus, any kind of hypothetical construct can be used to represent an energy concept, and the description of the hypothetical construct will, amongst other things, entail a description of the goal or end-state to which the energy is directed. Depending on how the goal or end-state is described, some energy concepts refer to physiological hypothetical constructs, whereas others refer to mentalistic or mechanistic hypothetical constructs. For example if the goal is a physiological state then the energy concept must refer to a physiological hypothetical construct. If the goal is a mechanistic state then the energy concept must refer to a mechanistic hypothetical construct.

There are numerous goals or end-states which have been suggested in the literature. Some goals refer to the attainment of external criteria such as money or painting a beautiful picture; others refer to the attainment of internal criteria such as 'balanced', 'congruent' or 'consonant' relations between cognitive elements, that is, between other hypothetical constructs. Some authors, such as McDougall (1908), suggest that there are very many energies or goals; others such as Freud suggest that there are relatively few, with much of behaviour providing indirect satisfaction for these few goals. Freud is distinctive in being the first psychologist to suggest that people are not consciously aware of what some of their goals are.

Since hypothetical constructs which have energising properties towards particular kinds of goal or end-state cannot be seen, there is sometimes disagreement over their existence or relevance to behaviour. For example, one of the most important differences between Freud and Jung is that Freud insisted that the sexual drive was paramount; Jung considered that the sexual drive was no more important than a number of other drives. One of the differences between the more modern humanistic type of psychologist and his more traditional behaviourist counterpart is that the former is concerned with existential needs such as self-actualisation, self-enhancement and the search for meaning, goals which are best represented mentalistically; the latter is concerned with more mundane needs such as hunger or thirst which are better represented physiologically or mechanistically.

A number of questions about energy concepts need to be explored. What energy concepts exist? What is the effect, if any, of not attaining the goal specified by the energy concept? What happens to the intensity of activity towards the satisfaction of one goal on the satisfaction of some other goal? Is there, for example, some central pool of energies or are the different energies quite separate? When constructing a theory it is often necessary to suggest at least tentative answers to these questions.

Directional concepts

Once an individual is motivated or energised to attain a particular goal, a second hypothetical construct can then be introduced to explain *how* that goal is achieved. This second hypothetical construct explains directionality, the direction taken to satisfy a goal from a set of available choice alternatives. The state of the hypothetical construct of a particular individual shows the choice he will or is likely to take. The hypothetical construct which has the function of explaining directionality can either be a physiological, mentalistic or mechanistic hypothetical construct and the choice alternatives must be expressed physiologically, mentalistically or mechanistically respectively. For example, directionality can be explained mentalistically by describing the *reason* of the behaving individual for carrying out his action. The reason of the behaving individual will specify situational characteristics specially selected by him to show that in terms of the 'logic of the situation' (which include accepted norms and rules of appropriateness) a particular choice alternative is a good way of attaining the goal. The reason of the behaving individual is a multidimensional hypothetical construct where the dimensions represent the different mentalistic criteria for adopting choices. Directionality can be explained mechanistically in terms of the concept of utility. The choice selected amongst a set of choice alternatives is that with the highest utility. Utility is a mechanistic hypothetical construct which functions within a system of mechanism. Another way of providing a mechanistic representation of directionality is to use the concept of a 'selector'. A selector is a hypothetical construct predetermined to direct behaviour towards alternatives on the basis of situational characteristics expressed within the context of a mechanical system.

Directionality is usually expressed in terms of mentalistic or mechanistic hypothetical constructs. Physiological hypothetical constructs are seldom used because choice alternatives are difficult to represent physiologically. Directionality, however, could be expressed physiologically. Suppose that there is a physiological learning substrate such as RNA which can be in one of two states, a 'turning left' state and a 'turning right' state. The RNA could be used to explain the direction taken by a rat in seeking to avoid hunger.

Choice between alternatives may be governed either by a single hypothetical construct whose states vary on a number of dimensions, or they may be governed by the states of a number of hypothetical constructs. For example, the decision to ask someone out for a date may be determined in part by one's attitude and in part by the likelihood that the person will accept. The most-favoured person may not be chosen for fear of rejection. When a choice alternative is governed by a multidimensional hypothetical construct, then different locations in the multidimensional matrix map different probabilities of accepting a particular choice. A description of the hypothetical construct involves specifying these probabilities. Where a choice alternative is governed by more than one hypothetical construct we must derive a formula which in some way adds the effects of the different hypothetical constructs. The important point to note is that when combinations of hypothetical constructs are used to determine directionality the hypothetical constructs must all be of the same kind. (If hypothetical constructs are not all of the same kind then there is the possibility that a factor could be added twice.) When any particular sort of directionality is explained through a multi-causal array of hypothetical constructs, then those hypothetical constructs must all be of the same kind.

Directional concepts, then, refer to hypothetical constructs which predict directionality from a set of choice alternatives. The direction chosen can be predicted from the state(s) of the hypothetical construct(s) and the availability of choice alternatives.

Performance concepts

Once an individual has decided what he wants to do he then has to set about doing it. Performance concepts are used to explain the difference or relation between what a person has chosen to do and what he actually does. Performance concepts explain how a particular choice alternative is realised and they are therefore used to explain limitations in human performance or skill. The performance concept refers to a hypothetical construct which corresponds to one particular choice alternative. The states of the hypothetical construct describe the different behavioural outcomes which occur, given that the individual is trying to attain the particular alternative. For example, when someone is performing a memory task his intention may be to learn all the nonsense syllables in the list. A performance concept is needed to explain how well he has learnt the list. The performance concept will be a hypothetical construct labelled 'memory' and the states of the hypothetical construct – for example, number of syllables learnt – correspond to different levels of performance. Performance concepts, then, refer to either uni- or multidimensional hypothetical constructs in which variation along the dimensions corresponds to changes in the level of performance. The hypothetical construct will be multidimensional (states vary along more than one dimension) when the skill entailed in performing the task has more than one component.

Performance concepts can refer to either physiological, mentalistic or mechanistic hypothetical constructs depending on the kind of performance one wishes to portray. Performance on any task, whether it is memorising, or bicycle riding, or bucket-making is best described by variation in the states of a mechanistic hypothetical construct, because such tasks are conveniently represented as outputs of a mechanistic system. Performance in reasoning or thinking, however, can be described either mechanistically or mentalistically. A mechanistic description of reasoning or behaviour in a problem-solving task involves a mechanistic hypothetical construct which can be in various states, such as a correct solution state and an incorrect solution state. Behaviour is explained in terms of how these different states are obtained. A mentalistic description of reasoning involves a description of the thoughts of the reasoning individual. Both the correct and incorrect solutions are thoughts, and reasoning is explained in terms of how other thoughts give rise to the correct or incorrect solution. Lastly, performance can also be described physiologically. A physiological hypothetical construct such as arousal can be used to describe performance on some simple motor task. The higher the state of arousal (within limits), the better the performance.

Notice that both directional concepts and performance concepts can involve choice. For example, in goal-orientated behaviour there is a choice between alternatives and in a performance task a choice between various solutions. What is the difference between directional and performance concepts? The difference lies in the consequences of choosing the different alternatives. In the case of a directional concept *any* alternative will achieve the desired goal or end-state. Hunger can be avoided by eating at any restaurant. However in the case of performance concepts, different choices, when they occur, do not result in the same consequences. One choice may be a correct solution, another incorrect. Thus directional concepts are used to describe how people intend to carry out particular kinds of action; performance concepts are used to describe the success with which those actions are achieved.

Use of and relation between energy, directional and performance concepts

Uses

Energy, directional and performance concepts each explain a different characteristic of behaviour. Energy concepts explain variation in the intensity of goal-orientated behaviour; directional concepts explain variation in its direction; and performance concepts explain the level or skill (in goal-orientated or non-goal-orientated behaviour). By saying that behaviour is explained, one means only that particular characteristics of behaviour are explained. Depending on the characteristics of the behaviour to be explained, one can use either an energy concept, a directional concept, a performance concept, or some combination of the three.

An energy concept should be used if there are variations in intensity of goal-orientated activity. If there are no fluctuations in the intensity of the goal-orientated behaviour and the goal or end-state is normal, then it may be unnecessary to specify what the goal or end-state is. Suppose a person is deciding which restaurant to go to, it is fairly clear that his goal or end-state is to avoid hunger, and so the energy concept is self-evident. When explaining his decision to go to one restaurant rather than another it may be (but need not be) unnecessary to specify the extent of his hunger. A directional concept should be introduced when there is some choice in the way a goal can be attained. If there are no choices then a directional concept will not be necessary. Consider a rat in a Skinner box pressing a lever to obtain food. The rat has no choice in how hunger is relieved because only food pellets are available and so when explaining the rat's behaviour in the box a directional concept will not be needed. A performance concept should be used when there is any discrepancy between a person's choice of action and the extent to which he achieves that action. A performance concept is used when variation in behaviour is determined by the skill of the individual. If skill is not needed to carry out a task, then a performance concept will not be needed. For example, going out to a restaurant does not involve much skill, so in explaining choice between restaurants a directional concept is needed, but not a performance concept. But if one wants to explain more than one characteristic of behaviour then it may be necessary to specify energy, directional and performance concepts. For example, the behaviour of an academic can be characterised by (a) the intensity with which he works, (b) the choice of subject he adopts, (c) his skill as an academic. To explain all these different characteristics of behaviour, it is necessary to include all three sorts of explanatory concept.

It was said earlier that one of the characteristics of behaviour is that it is often goal-orientated. Not all behaviour, however, is goal-orientated. Behaviour which is genetically determined, such as the releaser mechanism observed in animals and behaviour described as habits, do not have the characteristic of goal orientatedness. When explaining goal-orientated behaviour an account of the energy and directional concepts must be provided (though one of these may be self-evident or unnecessary). Explanations of behaviour which are not goal-orientated do not entail energy or directional concepts and are effected entirely in terms of hypothetical constructs having the explanatory function of a performance concept. Habits are behaviours which were once goal-orientated but where goal-orientatedness is no longer needed for the behaviour to occur. In order to explain a habit, one postulates a hypothetical construct having the explanatory function of a performance concept which directs behaviour in a certain predetermined and fixed manner. Whereas goal-orientated behaviour changes according to circumstances, habits are fixed and the hypothetical construct explaining the habit has a single value, which corresponds to the particular behaviour which occurs. Habits, then, are explained in terms of hypothetical constructs having the explanatory function of a performance concept.

Relations

What relation is there between hypothetical constructs having the different explanatory functions of energy concepts, directional concepts and performance concepts? Hypothetical constructs having different explanatory functions do not have causal relations between each other; they cannot do so as they explain different characteristics of behaviour which may be simultaneous. Instead, hypothetical constructs having different explanatory functions are located in different, parallel processes which cause a single behaviour, each hypothetical construct causing a different characteristic of that behaviour.

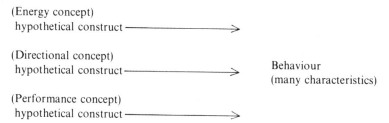

When hypothetical constructs having different explanatory functions form part of the same explanation (that is, explain the same behaviour) then the value of one hypothetical construct may *determine* the value of another. For example, the particular goals an individual tries to achieve will determine what choice of alternatives are open to him. They will determine what sets of choice alternatives he can choose from in order to achieve those goals. In other words, the values of an individual's energy concepts will determine the sort of directional concepts which should be employed in explaining his behaviour. At the same time the availability of a choice alternative will determine whether or not a goal is achieved and so the intensity of goal-orientated behaviour will be affected by the sorts of directions with which the individual can satisfy his goals. There may be available, for instance, choice alternatives which he prefers not to take. The alternative chosen by an individual to attain a goal determines the kinds of skills required to perform a task, but success at performance on the task may determine what alternatives a person chooses as well as whether or not the goal is achieved.

Although hypothetical constructs with different explanatory functions are located in different parallel processes, they are not independent: the value of one often determines the value of another. Hypothetical constructs having different explanatory functions are related when they explain a single behaviour. The different characteristics of a single behaviour are related and so naturally the concepts explaining those characteristics must also be related. However, because the relationship between hypothetical constructs having different explanatory functions stems from the relation between the characteristics of the behaviour they explain, the relationship is independent of the nature of those hypothetical constructs. Thus, hypothetical constructs having different explanatory functions which explain the same behaviour can consist of hypothetical constructs of either the same or different ontological status. For example, a behaviour which is explained using energy, directional and performance concepts may use physiological hypothetical constructs for the energy concept, mentalistic hypothetical constructs for the directional concept, and mechanistic hypothetical constructs for the performance concept. When behaviour is explained by more than one explanatory concept, the hypothetical constructs referred to by those explanatory concepts may have different natures.

EXPLANATORY CONCEPTS WHICH REFER TO DIFFERENCES, CHANGES OR RELATIONS AMONGST HYPOTHETICAL CONSTRUCTS

Individual Differences, Situational Differences and Interactionism

Research strategies in psychology can be divided into three categories. Nomothetic research seeks to establish how differences in situations cause differences in behaviour. Ideographic research seeks to establish consistent individual differences in behaviour. Interactionism, which is a comparatively new strategy, seeks to examine situation–individual interactions as determinants of behaviour. In this section the traditional ideographic approach, the traditional nomothetic approach and the interactionist approach will all be examined.

Ideographic psychology: personality concepts

Put two people in the same situation and they may behave quite differently: there are individual differences in behaviour. Many of these individual differences are relatively consistent in different situations and to explain this, personality concepts are introduced. The study of personality is the study of individual differences and transituational consistencies. The differences and consistencies which make up a personality concept should be relatively long term. Where they are short term they are referred to as mood or set.

Individual differences in behaviour occur either because hypothetical constructs are in different states or because operators have different forms. For the sake of conciseness only the former alternative will be discussed. The hypothetical constructs which are used to explain individual differences must, in order to constitute a dimension of personality, have sufficient generality to explain transituational consistencies, that is, they must explain behaviour in a number of situations. Any hypothetical construct, whether it has the function of either an energy, a directional, or a performance concept can be used to explain individual differences. The majority of current personality dimensions focus on directionality rather than some other aspect of behaviour. However one personality dimension which does describe variation in energy is the dimension manic–depressive. In the manic state the individual sets out to achieve grand and often impossible goals; his behaviour is intensely motivated towards a number of different goals. In the depressed state there is little behaviour and goal-orientated activity is low. Concepts of motivation such as need for achievement and need for affiliation are also sometimes introduced as personality dimensions and these also refer to variations in the state of a hypothetical construct having the function of an energy concept.

Most dimensions of personality reflect differences amongst hypothetical constructs having the explanatory function of directional concepts. Directional concepts tend to explain a more specific aspect of behaviour than energy concepts. Simply describing how a particular goal is achieved does not provide sufficient generality to achieve transituational consistency. Dimensions of personality are therefore similarities in choices *which are common to more than one goal*. Individual differences are explained in terms of differences between these similarities of choice or style of choosing.

There are many different characteristics of choice alternatives which can be selected to describe a dimension of personality. For example, in Eysenck's introvert/extravert dimension, the extravert is a stimulus seeker. Whenever the extravert satisfies a goal he will select a choice alternative which provides him with maximum stimulation. When working he will choose to do so in the presence of others and when relaxing he will choose to go to a party. The introvert, on the other hand, avoids stimulation. When he is working he will avoid the stimulation of others and he is more likely to relax at home. The goals of the introvert are achieved through choices which minimise stimulation. Those of the extravert are achieved through choices which maximise stimulation. Another example is the dominant–submissive dimension used by Cattell. The dominant individual chooses ways of achieving a goal or end-state which enables him to be dominant; the submissive individual chooses ways of achieving goals which enable him to be submissive. The dominant/submissive dimension, like all other personality traits, is a mechanistic representation of personality, in other words, personality is represented by mechanistic hypothetical constructs. Although many personality dimensions employ mechanistic hypothetical constructs, directionality can also be expressed through physiological or mentalistic hypothetical constructs. Eysenck's introversion/extraversion dimension can be described both mechanistically or physiologically – in terms of reactive inhibition. Kelly's personal constructs are ways of constructing the world. They are mentalistic hypothetical constructs which describe the way people judge things, judgments which form the basis of choice between alternatives. Personality dimensions can be based on differences between hypothetical constructs which are either physiological, mentalistic or mechanistic, and this option applies not only to hypothetical constructs which are directional concepts, but also to those which are energy concepts. In both cases, however, mechanistic hypothetical constructs are, at the moment, more frequently used than other kinds of hypothetical construct.

Differences in behaviour may also be caused by differences amongst performance concepts. Differences amongst performance concepts result in differences in behaviour which are more specific even than differences amongst directional concepts, and so differences amongst performance concepts often lack the ability to predict transituational consistencies. Individual differences in performance are usually just individual differences in particular skills and one cannot generalise from one skill to another. There is one important exception: many of the skills entailing rational thought are correlated, and these thinking skills or 'intelligence' are capable of predicting behaviour across many different situations, situations involving many different skills. Because these thinking skills are transituationally consistent, intelligence can be used as a personality concept. Intelligence does not describe differences in goal-orientatedness, it describes differences in ability. There is therefore just one personality concept which is at the same time a performance concept; that of intelligence.

In sum, the concept of personality is used to describe differences in behaviour which are consistent across situations. These differences can either be attributed to differences in the energies of goal-orientated activities; or to differences in styles of choosing between alternatives, styles which are consistent across more than one goal; or to differences in performance concepts relating to intellectual activity.

Nomothetic psychology, situational differences

One very obvious characteristic of behaviour is that it is often different in different situations. Such differences in behaviour are often consistently different in different situations. Behaviour at funerals is consistently different from behaviour at parties. Such consistent differences in behaviour can be explained by postulating that different situations affect hypothetical constructs differently. That is, different situations cause a particular hypothetical construct to be in different states. For example the funeral might cause a 'mood' hypothetical construct to be in a 'sad' state and the party may cause it to be in a 'happy' state.

It is interesting to note that there is no common term for a hypothetical construct which has the function of explaining differences between situations. Whereas individual differences are explained in terms of personality concepts, situational differences are explained in terms of hypothetical constructs which do not have a generic title of function. This absence of a descriptive label for concepts explaining situational differences is almost certainly due to the fact that inter-situational differences are so ubiquitous in psychology; however it is worth observing that there is a terminological imbalance between concepts explaining individual and situational differences.

Any hypothetical construct can be used to explain differences in behaviour in different situations. A hypothetical construct which has the function of an energy concept would explain why there are differences in the intensity of goal-seeking behaviour in different situations. A hypothetical construct which has the function of a directional concept would explain why individuals choose differently in different situations. A hypothetical construct which has the function of a performance concept would explain why individuals perform at a task better or worse in different situations. A hypothetical construct having any function or for that matter any nature can be used to explain differences in behaviour in different situations. One characteristic of these hypothetical constructs which explain differences in behaviour in different situations is that it is generally assumed that they, and hence the differences in behaviour, are consistent across different individuals. One expects everyone, or at least the majority of individuals, to be sad at funerals and happy at parties. One of the assumptions in the traditional nomothetic approach is that where differences in behaviour occur between situations then those differences will be relatively consistent across different individuals.

Interactionism

Interactionism, which can be traced back to the early proponents of theoretical psychology such as Lewin (Ekehammar, 1974), takes the approach that behaviour is caused by both the situation and the individual. So, in order to predict behaviour it is necessary to take both situational and individual variables into account (Bowers, 1973; Mischel, 1973; Bem and Allen, 1974; Endler and Magnusson, 1976). According to the interactionist viewpoint behaviour is characterised by both individual differences and situational differences, and these differences often interact. For example, the way a situation affects an individual depends on the sort of individual being affected; conversely, the order of individual differences amongst a population depends on the situation in which those individual differences are measured.

An important point to realise is that both individual differences, situational differences, and interactions can be explained through the use of one and the same hypothetical construct. It is not necessary to postulate a special individual-differences-explaining hypothetical construct and a special situational-differences-explaining hypothetical construct and a special interaction-explaining-hypothetical construct. Differences in the state of a hypothetical construct can be used to explain any sort of difference of behaviour.

An example of a hypothetical construct which has been used to explain both situational and individual differences is the construct Belief in a Just World (Lerner and Simmons, 1966; Lerner and Matthews, 1967). The Belief in a Just World construct was first formulated to explain differences in behaviour in different situations such as why innocent victims are derogated more than guilty victims. Later Rubin and Peplau (1973) reasoned that there should be individual differences in the extent to which people believe that they live in a just world and so developed the Just World scale. Other research (for example, Zuckerman, 1975) has demonstrated interactions between situations and individuals measured on the Just World scale. Thus, the Belief in a Just World construct has been used to explain both situational differences, individual differences and interactions.

There are however certain constraints on the use of hypothetical constructs which explain situational and individual differences. A hypothetical construct which functions as a personality concept is assumed to be consistent across different situations. If that same hypothetical construct is to explain differences between situations, then the situations between which it explains a difference must be different from those situations across which it is consistent. A hypothetical construct which is used to explain both individual differences and situational differences will be constrained with respect to the particular sort of differences it explains.

The presence of an interaction indicates that the situation is related by a complex operator to the hypothetical construct caused by the situation. The resulting state of the hypothetical construct depends not only on the situation but also on the initial state of the hypothetical construct. The idea of an interaction will be examined in more detail and from an empirical point of view in the next chapter (see also pp. 80–1).

Learning concepts

The concept of learning is introduced to explain a characteristic of behaviour involving change. Some situations cause long-term changes in behaviour which remain longer than the duration of the situation causing the change. These long-term changes in behaviour are explained in terms of long-term changes in the state of a hypothetical construct or changes in the connections between hypothetical constructs (that is, a change in the form of an operator). Learning is not a hypothetical construct; learning is something which happens to hypothetical constructs; it is a long-term change amongst hypothetical constructs which is caused by a situation.

For learning to occur there must be some change amongst hypothetical constructs. When learning occurs it is possible that a hypothetical construct having the function either of an energy concept, a directional concept or a performance concept can change. For example, the achievement motive can be learnt through early independence training. That is, the value of the energy concept which directs behaviour towards the goal of achievement is changed through early independence training. Learning can also affect hypothetical constructs which have the function of directional concepts. For instance, attitudes are learnt dispositions towards objects and positive and negative interactions will lead to change in attitude towards the object. Performance concepts can also be changed through learning. Memory is a hypothetical construct which is changed by interaction with learning situations. Skill in reasoning can be improved by certain educational programmes.

The explanatory concept of learning, then, refers to a long-term change amongst hypothetical constructs, hypothetical constructs having the explanatory function of either energy, directional, or performance concepts. It is interesting to realise that *every* hypothetical construct and *every* operator has the state or form it has either because it is genetically determined or because it is learnt. It would therefore be unusual for the explanatory concept of learning *not* to feature in explanations of behaviour.

Perception concepts

Some authors have argued that the individual's perception of his situation, his 'psychological situation', is a better predictor of behaviour than some 'objective' assessment of the situation by outside observers (for example, Koffka, 1935; Lewin, 1936, 1938; Murray, 1938). It may therefore be advantageous to introduce an internal representation of the situation into a theory, an internal representation which mediates between the real situation and other hypothetical constructs. The psychological situation or perceived situation is a hypothetical construct, which can be of any kind depending on the sort of internal representation which is required; the consequences of relating each of the three kinds of hypothetical construct to the situation has been discussed in chapter 5. Perception concepts are introduced to explain the relation or difference or change between situations and internal representations of situations. Perception concepts refer to the relation between the situation and a hypothetical construct, a hypothetical construct which is caused by the situation and is some form of representation of the situation. Perception concepts refer to operators, and when one says that there is a change in perception one means that the form of the operator has changed.

Perception concepts are used to explain two sorts of discrepancy between situations and internal representations of situations. One is long term, stable discrepancies between situations and hypothetical constructs; the other is, transitory variation in the extent of change an aspect of the situation causes in a hypothetical construct. The former sort of discrepancy entails biases such as those found in the visual illusions. Visual illusions represent stable discrepancies between an 'objective' assessment of the world and some internal representation. Another example of stable discrepancies are biases in the judgment of situations, biases referred to as motivated perception. The second sort of discrepancy is associated with the study of attention. The amount of causal influence an aspect of the situation has in changing a hypothetical construct can vary. Attended stimuli cause greater change than unattended stimuli; indeed unattended stimuli may cause no change whatever in the states of a hypothetical construct. The perception concept of attention, then, is used to describe the extent of causal influence that different aspects of the situation have on a hypothetical construct.

To understand perception concepts they must be placed in relation to other explanatory concepts – energy concepts, directional concepts, and performance concepts. The hypothetical constructs which are referred to by these other explanatory concepts each have a causal relation with the situation (figure 8.1).

Different aspects of the situation are causally relevant to hypothetical constructs having different explanatory functions. For

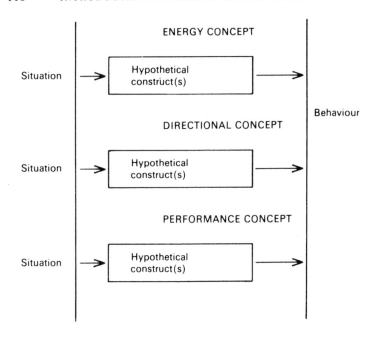

Figure 8.1

example the time since last eating is relevant to the intensity of hunger and hence to a hypothetical construct which has the function of an energy concept. The choice of available restaurants is relevant to a hypothetical construct which has the function of a directional component. The clues used to solve a problem are relevant to a hypothetical construct which has the function of a performance concept. Thus, different aspects of the situation have a causal influence on hypothetical constructs with different explanatory functions. Each of these different situation/hypothetical construct relations may be described by a perception concept, but they only need to be described by a perception concept when there is some sort of discrepancy between the situation and the hypothetical construct: when there is no discrepancy then a perception concept will be unnecessary. For example, a perception concept will be needed to explain why a person is not feeling hungry when, having had no food for twelve hours, he watches an exciting football game. A perception concept would not be necessary if the individual was feeling hungry after twelve hours' food deprivation. A perception concept will be needed to explain why, when making a choice of restaurants, the little one with the uninteresting sign is not noticed. A perception concept will not be needed if one is aware of all choice alternatives. A perception concept will be needed to explain shift of attention in a signal-detecting task, but if no shift occurs then the perception concept will not be necessary.

In sum, perception concepts are used to describe *some* of the relations between situations and hypothetical constructs, hypothetical constructs which can either be energy, directional or performance concepts. Each hypothetical construct or group of hypothetical constructs which has a different explanatory function must have its own causal relation with the situation. Some of the causal relations, those involving discrepancies, call for the use of a perception concept; others do not.

Combinations of explanatory concepts: perceptual learning and motivated perception

Perceptual bias and patterns of attention can arise for one or both of two reasons. They can either be genetically determined, or they can be learnt. Some visual illusions based on interactions between orientation detectors are genetically determined. On the other hand, Gregory suggests that the Müller–Lyer illusion reflects learning of perspective. When the relation between the situation and a hypothetical construct is learnt, then one refers to perceptual learning.

Change in perceptual bias or attention can be caused (indirectly) by other hypothetical constructs, ones which will either be energy, directional or performance concepts. A hypothetical construct can have an indirect causal relation with an operator through the device of identification between operators and hypothetical constructs: the 'causing' hypothetical construct causes some other hypothetical construct which is identified with the operator (see chapter 7). When the operator referred to by the perception concept is indirectly caused by a hypothetical construct which is an energy or directional concept then one speaks of motivated perception or attention being directed at will. The biases in perception and direction of attention are both goal-orientated. When the operator referred to by the perceptual concept is indirectly caused by a performance concept, then the perception is being directed through some aspect of skill. Thus, hypothetical constructs which are either energy, directional or performance concepts can, indirectly, cause changes in the form of the operator which is a perception concept.

Conclusion: Explanatory concepts

The preceding description of explanatory concepts has been extremely sketchy. This is because analysis of explanatory concepts and how they are realised in terms of hypothetical constructs and operators is still at a very elementary stage. However, even with this elementary analysis there is a very important lesson to be learnt: one should not expect a hypothetical construct to do too much. A hypothetical construct, or for that matter a group of hypothetical constructs, cannot be expected to explain all the characteristics of behaviour, only some of them.

Some theories have been criticised on the grounds that they do not explain this or that characteristic of behaviour. For example, Heider's theory of balance (Heider, 1958) has been criticised on the grounds that it does not predict which attitudes in an unbalanced triad are likely to change. The frustration–aggression hypothesis has been criticised on the grounds that it does not predict the direction of displacement; it does not predict the target which is used as a scapegoat. A little consideration will show why these two theories have these limitations. Both theories introduce energy concepts, but they do not include directional concepts. As a consequence the theories can explain variation in intensity but not in directionality. This is a limitation rather than a weakness of these theories as both can easily be extended to explain directionality, though that naturally would entail the introduction of new hypothetical constructs. A theory need not explain all characteristics of behaviour; it need only explain some of them. Nevertheless, to avoid raising false hopes and possible misunderstandings it is as well to specify what those characteristics are. The first thing to do when constructing a theory is to say what the theory is intended to explain.

SITUATIONS IN WHICH THE BEHAVIOUR TO BE EXPLAINED OCCURS

As has been remarked earlier, there are three ways or criteria which can be used to separate the different areas in psychology: (a) the kind of explanation provided; (*b*) characteristics of the behaviour which is to be explained; and (*c*) characteristics of the situation in which the behaviour to be explained occurs. To summarise, the first criterion bases its separation on the use of different kinds of hypothetical construct and divides psychology into *kinds* of psychology. The different kinds of psychology are (*a*) physiological psychology or psychophysiology, (*b*) phenomenological, existential or humanistic psychology, and (*c*) cognitive psychology. The second criterion bases its separation on the use of different sorts of explanatory concept and divides psychology into different *topics*, such as motivation, performance, learning, personality and perception.

Both these criteria have in the past led to an over-compartmentalisation of ideas in psychology but they do, nevertheless, provide us with a way of classifying and understanding theories. They are both useful criteria because they help us describe and represent theories systematically. The third criterion – characteristics of the situation in which the behaviour to be explained occurs – does not have this useful theoretical function and although it will be of interest to politicians and grant-awarding bodies, it has little relevance to the theoretical psychologist.

This third criterion divides psychology into areas of study on the basis of different kinds of situation and so divides psychology into areas of application. These areas of application include occupational psychology, educational psychology, clinical or abnormal psychology, environmental psychology and social psychology. All these different applications of psychology are distinguished by the situation causing the behaviour – at work, in school, in hospital, people together. The reason why differences of application are not relevant to the theoretical psychologist is that theories and theoretical concepts are not specific to situations, they are not specific to particular areas of application. Indeed, the whole point of a theory as opposed to an empirical generalisation is that it should apply in different situations. For example, a theory about the social behaviour of man may be useful in explaining behaviour in an occupational setting. Abnormalities amongst the states of hypothetical constructs in this theory may explain some aspect of abnormal behaviour and the learning of these abnormalities may be classified within the area of developmental or educational psychology. So theoretical ideas are not specific to different areas of application though, naturally, the way the theoretical idea is applied, that is, the particular situation causing the behaviour, will differ between these different areas. Because differences in application do not provide any insight into the nature of theories in psychology, they do not form part of our conceptual framework used for systematising theories.

Theories in psychology have now been examined from a number of different perspectives. Theories in psychology show how behaviour is the result of certain individual and situational characteristics. Individual characteristics have been considered in terms of the nature of the theoretical concepts used, and characteristics of the behaviour to be explained in terms of explanatory concepts. Brief mention has been made of the different situations in which behaviour occurs. So far this book has been concerned with the construction of psychological theories; the final chapter examines how to test them.

9 Testing Theories

A theory is a way of describing how the world works. When a theory is constructed, a guess is made about how the world works and then this guess is described in theoretical terms. Of course, people have always made guesses about the world they live in. Superstitious beliefs are a case in point and superstitious beliefs existed long before the development of scientific theories. The difference between the guess involved in superstitious beliefs and the guess in scientific theories is that some attempt is made to establish the truth of the scientific guess through a process of *testing*. A guess is scientific by virtue of the fact that an attempt is made to find out, on the basis of observation, whether or not it is true. In the case of non-scientific guesses, no attempt is made to see whether the guess is true, indeed it may not even be possible to tell from observation whether the guess is true or false.

It is worth reflecting that although data can exist without theories (empirical generalisations) one cannot have scientific theories without data as the truth of a theory, whether or not the theory is correct, depends on data. Theoretical psychology should not be interpreted as a kind of armchair speculation divorced from observation. Theories and data must always interrelate: untested (or untestable) theories are little different from superstitions.

Confidence in the truth of a theory is established through a process of testing. One characteristic of theories is that they predict the occurrence of observable events. On the basis of any particular theory it is possible to predict the occurrence of a particular event or a singular occurrence. If the predicted singular occurrence occurs and the observable event is in accordance with the predictions of the theory, then one can feel more confident that that theory is true.

If the observed singular occurrences are different from the theory's predictions, then the conclusion is that the theory is false. The crux of the matter is that the truth of a theory can only be established with a certain level of confidence; a theory can never be *proved* to be true.

There may be many singular occurrences which are consistent with the theory's predictions, but there is always the possibility that a singular occurrence will turn up later on which goes against the theory's prediction. The previous consistency between observation and prediction may have been the result of a lucky chance rather than because the theory was true. So, however many singular occurrences which are favourable to the theory have been observed, it can never be said with absolute certainty that the theory is true. But if a large number of singular occurrences have been observed, all of which have been consistent with the theory's predictions, then it is unlikely that so much consistency between observation and prediction would have occurred by chance. It is then justifiable to conclude that the theory is correct, or to have a high degree of confidence that the theory is correct. Technically speaking, a theory is confirmed or corroborated, it is not proved.

A theory is tested either by setting up conditions and observing outcomes (as in an experiment) or by observing events (as in non-experimental tests) which are relevant to that theory's predictions. A test provides favourable evidence for the theory if the observations are consistent with the theory's predictions, and unfavourable evidence if the observations are inconsistent with the theory's predictions. The most important point about a test is that favourable evidence can only be concluded from a particular procedure *if it would have been possible to have obtained unfavourable evidence.* Procedures which cannot produce unfavourable evidence whatever the outcome do not test a theory. Such procedures may contribute to our store of empirical knowledge, but they do not contribute to our understanding of theories, since they do not, in any way, confirm or corroborate the theory. For example, if there are two possible outcomes from an experiment, each of which can be interpreted as being consistent with the predictions of a theory, then that experiment does not test the theory, and whatever result is obtained it provides neither favourable nor unfavourable evidence for the theory.

In psychological research, there is a tendency when testing a theory to consider only the events a theory predicts will occur. However, a more useful approach to the design of empirical research might be to consider what data a theory predicts should not occur. By considering such data one is less likely to arrive at a procedure which is incapable of producing unfavourable evidence. A test must have the possibility of showing the theory to be false.

Unless a theory is well established, it is usually the case that there are a number of competing theories which can be used to explain a particular sort of phenomenon. Each of these competing theories is confirmed or corroborated by the extent to which its predictions are consistent with the observed data. Sometimes different theories will make the same predictions about data and when similar predictions occur, tests of such data will not discriminate between the truth content of the different theories. So, if there are a number of competing theories, it is important to seek and test predictions which are different for different theories. Although different theories may sometimes make the same predictions about data, there must be some predictions which are different – otherwise the theories could be considered identical. Data which is capable of discriminating between predictions of different theories forms the basis of *critical tests*. Critical tests are tests which can be used to compare the truth of different theories. As is often the case, there are competing theories in psychology and the design or discovery of critical tests is very important. Theories should not be evaluated *in vacuo*, but in relation to other competing theories. A theory is confirmed by finding favourable evidence, but greater confirmation or corroboration for a theory is obtained by a finding which falsifies some other theory. If a finding corroborates one theory and falsifies another then this reduces the likelihood that the corroborating evidence for the first has occurred by chance, that it has occurred even though some other theory is in fact correct. However, at the risk of over-emphasising the point, even critical tests do not prove a theory; they merely contribute more to our confidence that the theory is correct.

One early suggestion in the literature on the philosophy of science is that a theory should be rejected once unfavourable evidence is discovered. Current opinion (Lakatos, 1971) holds that unfavourable evidence or anomalies do not necessarily lead to a theory's rejection, but may lead to a change or development in the theory so as to accommodate the new information. Unfavourable evidence need not be the end of a theory – it may lead to an improvement or sophistication of the theory. It is only if the theory cannot be changed to accommodate unfavourable data that the theory should be discarded. It may also happen that repeated theoretical change leads to a weakening of the empirical content of a theory, that is, repeated modification may make it difficult to find any unfavourable evidence whatsoever. If a theory has been much modified, it is worth considering whether the theory is still capable of useful prediction. If the empirical content is too small, it is hardly worth continuing to test the theory, as that theory will, in any event, be incapable of useful or useable predictions.

FROM THEORIES TO DATA

There are two sorts of procedure which need to be understood before setting out to obtain favourable or unfavourable evidence for a theory: (a) how to observe, describe and interpret observables or data; (b) how to deduce predictions about data from theories. The first of these procedures, observation, description and interpretation of data, is covered in the study of statistics and experimental design. A knowledge of statistics enables description of characteristics of data, characteristics which allow one to interpret relations between observables. Through the use of statistical techniques, one can determine, for example, the probability that two sets of data are obtained from the same sample, the extent to which two or more sets of data are correlated, and differences between the variance or the distribution of different sets of data. Any interpretation of data is statistical, that is, the truth of an interpretation is never known with absolute certainty; it is only possible to say that there is a certain probability that a particular relation between observables is true. The point to note is that theory confirmation entails two sorts of uncertainty. Uncertainty in the interpretation of data, and un-certainty because any piece of data, even though it is correctly interpreted, only confirms but does not prove the theory. Statistics provide a way of assessing to what extent interpretations of data are correct, but these interpretations are then used to assess the truth of a theory.

Collecting, describing and interpreting data is one part of theory testing. The second part entails working out what predictions a theory makes about data. These two procedures are not independent because the sort of predictions a theory makes depends on the way the data are to be collected. This section examines how conclusions can be drawn from data, doing so with reference to the different sorts of data which can be collected.

Any theory will make a number of predictions about behaviour. Some of these predictions are characteristics of the behaviour the theory was set up to explain; others may be about quite different behaviours. When testing a theory, any prediction can be used as the basis for a test; it is not necessary to stick to the predictions about the behaviour the theory was intended to explain. Other indirect tests can be used and these other indirect tests may form a valuable way of distinguishing between competing theories. When trying to establish the truth of a theory, it is best to test as many predictions as possible. The more predictions that are tested and lead to favourable evidence, the greater the confirmation for the theory.

Experimental and Non-experimental Paradigms

There are many ways in which data can be collected to test a theory. The data can come from an experiment where the experimenter manipulates independent variables and measures the outcome of such manipulation on dependent variables. Alternatively, the data can be collected from some non-experimental setting where the experimenter does not manipulate variables, but simply measures behaviours as they occur. The data can be collected in a laboratory, where the laboratory is designed to approximate to a greater or lesser extent to conditions in the outside world, or data can be collected outside the laboratory. Both these different methods of collecting data have their own particular advantages and disadvantages, but it must never be forgotten that they can *all* be used to test a theory. When testing a theory empirical data does not have to be restricted to just one kind of test. Any test, so long as it is a good one, can contribute to an understanding of theories, whether inside the laboratory or outside, whether experimental or non-experimental.

Although any procedure can be used to test a theory, different procedures have different characteristics. The use of either experimental or non-experimental paradigms tends to bias the sorts of factors which are investigated. In an experiment it is comparatively simpler or easier to manipulate situations rather than individuals. The experimental manipulation is almost synonymous with a comparison of the affects of different situations. Individual differences can be achieved through experimental manipulation but this usually involves procedures which are indirect and based on theoretical assumptions. For example, in his study of achievement motivation McClelland (McClelland *et al.*, 1953) manipulated the extent of achievement motivation of individuals by placing them in situations of different achievement-orientatedness and *assuming* that the different situations produced different sorts of individual. Manipulations of individual factors entail theoretical assumptions. However, manipulations of situations for the sake of comparing situation effects do not involve such assumptions.

Non-experimental paradigms usually entail correlations between two or more variables. That is, the analysis of non-experimental paradigms entails correlating individual differences along one variable with individual differences along some other variable. As a consequence non-experimental paradigms tend to be associated with the study of individual differences. Experimental studies, on the other hand, tend to be associated with the study of situational differences. These biases are by no means a necessary feature of either sort of paradigm but they do characterise current research in either experimental or non-experimental paradigms.

Predictions about Causality

A theory will make many predictions about observables, but almost all of them can be described as predictions about causality – predictions about causal relations between observables. Data collection, therefore, almost invariably entails finding out what causal connections, if any, do in fact occur. The aim of data collection when testing a theory is usually to establish causal connections. Data collected through experimentation has one important advantage over non-experimental data: in an experiment it is possible to establish precisely what causal relations between observables are occurring. To take an example, suppose an experiment involves one independent variable consisting of a control and experimental condition and one dependent variable. Suppose that different values of the dependent variable are obtained in the control and experimental conditions. There is then an unambiguous causal connection between the independent and dependent variables; change in the independent variable causes a change in the dependent variable and there is no other possible interpretation of the data within that particular paradigm. Non-experimental studies do not give such a clear indication about causal relations between observables, because they can only reveal statistical dependencies between observables (for example, correlations). The finding of statistical dependencies between two observables shows that there must be some kind of causal connection between them, but the statistical dependency does not necessarily make clear what form this causal connection takes. If a correlation is found between two variables, then either one is causing the other or they are both the consequence of some common cause: the correlation does not reveal which is true. There are, however, statistical techniques which do provide some information about causal connections between variables demonstrating statistical dependency, and this information is provided on the basis of assumptions about the relationship between causality and characteristics of correlated data (factor analysis, principal component analysis, partial correlation, etc.). Although experiments have the facility *par excellence* of establishing causal connections between observables, experiments do not have a monopoly. Non-experimental studies can discover causal relations, but by techniques which are indirect and sometimes open to criticism. (For a discussion of causality and non-experimental paradigms, see for example Blalock (1967, 1968), Harman (1967).)

A less direct way of testing predictions about causality involves the idea of an interaction. The idea of an interaction is best illustrated with an example. Imagine making wine: there is a gallon glass jar fitted with an air lock so that the rate of gas production can be observed. Carbon dioxide is produced, so the theory has it, because of yeast living in the developing wine. From a knowledge of yeast it can be predicted and also observed that the rate of gas production is influenced by two factors: (a) the temperature of the wine, and (b) the concentration of sugar. Either through observation of spontaneous change or through experimental manipulation, it is found that warm temperatures cause a faster production of gas than low temperatures. Also, high concentrations of sugar cause a faster production of gas than low concentrations. However, if the two factors temperature and sugar concentration are taken together an interesting observation can be made. *Either* low temperature *or* low sugar concentration, irrespective of the value of the other factor, will result in low gas production. The two factors are not independent; high sugar concentration or high temperature do not always cause high or even moderate levels of gas production. The effects of sugar concentration and temperature are not additive. The relationship between temperature, sugar concentration and gas production can be represented in

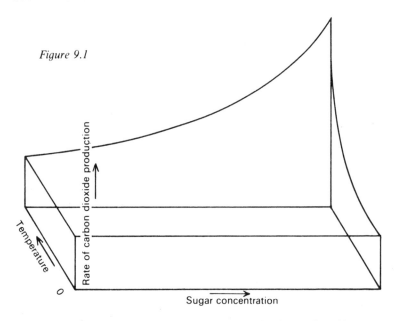

Figure 9.1

Rate of carbon dioxide production

Temperature

O

Sugar concentration

the form of the 3-dimensional graph shown in figure 9.1. (Assume that the temperature does not go above about 40° C.)

The 3-dimensional graph plots a curved surface. The surface could be detected as being curved by statistical tests such as analysis of variance. In an analysis of variance the effects of the two factors would interact or would be non-additive when the surface of the graph is curved rather than flat or sloping. The reason why temperature and sugar concentration interact is because they both affect the same agent of gas production. Yeast is affected both by temperature and sugar concentration and where an agent is affected by two factors, then the two factors would be expected to interact. If, on the other hand, there were a number of different agents of gas production, some affected by temperature but not sugar concentration, and others affected by sugar concentration but not temperature, then an interaction would not be expected. The effects of the separate factors would be independent and additive. In the case of wine making, an interaction between temperature and sugar concentration is predicted and observed because there is only one agent (yeast) causing the production of gas and this one agent is affected by both temperature and sugar concentration.

In psychology, independent variables interact (that is, when affecting a dependent variable) when the independent variables have a causal relation with the same hypothetical construct, a hypothetical construct which is measured by the dependent variable. So, if one postulates a hypothetical construct and the kind of observables which should cause changes in that hypothetical construct are known, then one should expect those observables or 'factors' to interact in measures of the hypothetical construct. If these observables or factors do not interact then there would seem to be some error in our suggestion of the hypothetical construct. The presence of an interaction can therefore be used as favourable evidence for a particular hypothetical construct.

The difference between factors which add and factors which interact has been used by Sternberg (1969) as a criterion for distinguishing the number of stages in a process, that is, the number of hypothetical constructs in a process. Sternberg applies his argument to the study of stages in a reaction-time task. He suggests that if two factors interact, then this can be taken as evidence that the two factors have a causal effect on the same stage. If two factors do not interact, but are additive, then this is evidence that the two factors affect different stages; and so the number of additive factors indicates the number of stages in a process. Sternberg represents his argument schematically, as shown in figure 9.2.

Sternberg's argument applies where the dependent variable is time – reaction time in his case. A quantification of the dimension of time is not being considered in this book. However, his argument does apply in a modified form to interactions on other dependent variables. If there is a sequence of hypothetical constructs which is caused by various factors, two of which cause the same hypothetical construct to change, then those two factors must interact in any measure of that change, irrespective of what that change happens to be. The absence of an interaction indicates that the two factors influence different hypothetical constructs. However, the presence of an interaction does not necessarily mean that two factors cause the same hypothetical construct. Consider the following example of two hypothetical constructs, each caused by different factors

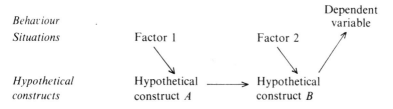

			Dependent
Behaviour			variable
Situations	Factor 1	Factor 2	

| *Hypothetical* | Hypothetical ⟶ | Hypothetical | |
| *constructs* | construct *A* | construct *B* | |

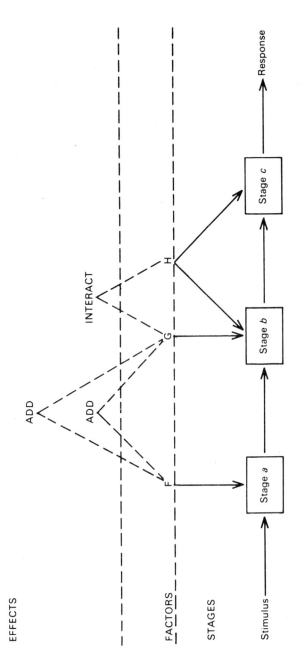

Figure 9.2 Relationship between factors, stages and presence or absence of interaction (from Sternberg, 1969)

Suppose that the dependent variable is time, being made up of the time to change hypothetical construct A and the time in which hypothetical construct B changes. Any change in the time hypothetical construct A changes is going to have no effect whatsoever on the time taken for hypothetical construct B to change. Time is not a state of a hypothetical construct and so it is not something which can act as a cause. So, with time as the dependent variable, the two factors must be independent and so additive. However, suppose that hypothetical construct B varies on dimension X and factor 2 causes a change on dimension X. Suppose further, that factor 1 causes a change in hypothetical construct A and this change in hypothetical construct A also causes a change on dimension X of hypothetical construct B. The effect of factor 1 on hypothetical construct B is now the same as the effect of factor 2 on hypothetical construct B, except that it is mediated through hypothetical construct A. But because factor 1 indirectly causes a change on the *same* dimension as the change caused by factor 2, the two factors will interact in any measure of the change in hypothetical construct B. So, although factor 1 and factor 2 are causally related to different hypothetical constructs, they will interact if certain conditions are met. They will interact if indirectly or directly their effects cause the same kind of change. They will not interact if indirectly or directly their effects do not cause the same kind of change. The conclusion is that factors which are additive provide evidence for separateness of hypothetical constructs. If there are N additive factors, then there must be at least N hypothetical constructs which cause the dependent variable. (The N hypothetical constructs need not, incidentally, be placed in a sequence.) If, on the other hand, different factors interact, then *either* the factors cause the same hypothetical construct *or* they cause different hypothetical constructs which are related in the way described above.

From a theoretical point of view, factors which add are often more interesting than factors which interact, as it is possible to draw more definite conclusions from additive factors. The only problem is that a conclusion to the effect that factors are additive is usually drawn from the finding that factors do not interact. Statistically, the finding that two factors interact is usually based on a rejection of the null hypothesis. The finding that two factors are additive generally means an acceptance of the null hypothesis. There is a general statistical principle that the likelihood of the null hypothesis being correct cannot be estimated statistically, so it is seldom possible to estimate the probability that two factors are additive. Therefore when one concludes from some data that two factors are additive, one has to be careful that one is not making a Type 2 error – the error of concluding that there is no effect when in fact there is one. There may not be an effect simply because of poor experimental procedure.

Of course, not all predictions made by theories are predictions about causal relations between observables. If a theory includes an identity relation between two hypothetical constructs then one would expect a correlation between measures of these two hypothetical constructs. Identity relations in theories are tested through an assessment of correlations. Observables caused by identified (and hence simultaneous) hypothetical constructs must covary. If the observables which are used to measure two identified hypothetical constructs are accurate measures of the hypothetical constructs, then the correlation would be expected to be quite high, but if either measure only approximates to the value of the hypothetical construct, then the correlation may be low.

Difficulties in Extrapolating from Data

One problem which seems to be peculiar to the science of psychology is that for any individual there are many processes which occur, and these different processes cannot be isolated very easily. One cannot divide up a person into little bits and be sure that one is studying a single bit in isolation. When studying just one bit or process one can never be sure that the results are not being influenced or contaminated by some other process. Although it is possible rigorously to control some external conditions, it is not possible to do likewise with internal conditions. Internal conditions can, at best, only be controlled indirectly. Extrapolation between data and theory has, therefore, the additional problem that findings may be attributable to a process other than the one under consideration. If an effect is obtained which is contrary to the predictions of a theory, it may be that the effect can be attributed to some other process. Suppose, for example, that there are two competing theories of prejudice, one of which predicts a positive correlation between prejudice and anxiety on the basis that anxiety causes prejudice, and another which makes no prediction about the relation between prejudice and anxiety at all.

If a positive correlation between prejudice and anxiety is found, then such data should only be interpreted as very weakly supporting the first rather than the second theory. The positive correlation, after all, may be occurring for some reason other than the formation of prejudice. There may be some causal factor which contributes both to the formation of prejudice and to the formation of anxiety. Hence a positive correlation between prejudice and anxiety could be found, even though the 'true' theory of prejudice does not make that prediction. However, such findings which may appear, quite incorrectly, inconsistent with a theory are more likely to occur when data is collected through a non-experimental procedure, although examples could be found from experimental data. A finding which is *not* predicted by a process does not necessarily constitute unfavourable evidence for that process if it could be explained through some other process, that is, a second process whose existence is compatible with the existence of the first.

The possibility that more than one process is operating at the same time introduces another problem into data interpretation. Suppose, again, there are two competing theories to explain the formation of prejudice. There is no reason why both theories may not be correct in the sense that the processes described in each theory contribute to the formation of prejudice. Suppose that both theories are correct and that a critical test is used to evaluate which of the two is correct. The evidence may well favour the stronger process, that is, the process which contributes more to prejudice, but this does not mean that the weaker process does not occur or even is unimportant to the formation of prejudice. Where two separate processes lead to the same behaviour it may be difficult to establish the relative effectiveness of the different processes.

Such problems in the interpretation of data arise because psychological processes cannot be isolated. One cannot be sure of studying a process in isolation. There seems to be only one way to obviate these problems: a theory or process should be tested not by one, but by many different kinds of procedure. The more various the ways that theories are evaluated the more evidence there is for accepting or rejecting theories, and the less likely it is that the conclusions are incorrect.

Saying that a theory provides a correct explanation of behaviour means that the process described in the theory occurs when the behaviour to be explained occurs, not that the process occurs all the time. The possibility that a process may function in some situations and not in others has been recognised for some time. Freud, in 1921, was one of the first to suggest that the psychological processes which occur when an individual is alone may be quite different from the psychological processes which occur when in a group. If psychological processes can occur in some situations and not others, then the evidence for those processes will only be found in some situations and not in others. One argument against the use of laboratory studies is that the laboratory is a special kind of situation, and the processes of interest may not occur in a laboratory setting. To look only to laboratory studies for data collection may lead to a false picture of psychological processes. Of course, it is not only laboratory studies which may bias the kind of process which takes place; any sort of obtrusive measure may alter the occurrence of psychological processes whether the person is in the laboratory or in some real-life setting. Not all processes, however, are situation specific and those processes which occur both in real-life settings as well as in the laboratory can be investigated just as well in the laboratory. After all, laboratories can vary to the extent to which they approximate to real life and some laboratory settings can be very realistic. Use of laboratories cannot be ruled out merely on the grounds that there is a possibility that they contaminate psychological processes. However, although there may be reasons for supposing that a process is or is not changed when the individual is placed in a laboratory setting, such conclusions must ultimately be based on empirical evidence.

Although laboratories have the disadvantage that processes occurring in a laboratory setting may differ from those occurring in real life, laboratories do have an important advantage. Laboratories provide a controlled setting where it is possible to manipulate variables independently of each other. Laboratories provide ideal conditions for carrying out experiments, and as stated before, experiments provide one of the best techniques for establishing causal relations. However, in certain cases experiments can be carried out in non-laboratory settings, though 'real-life experiments' are always more difficult to effect and there may be ethical reservations about involving people in procedures which they may have not voluntarily agreed to experience.

The possibility that processes are situation specific means that theories should, as far as possible, be tested in different situations. It was said earlier that greater confirmation for a theory is obtained when there are many different kinds of favourable evidence. These different kinds of favourable evidence should entail, amongst other things, tests in different situations. If a theory is tested in only one kind of situation then one should be a little cautious in extrapolating the findings to other situations. Not that this caveat should be taken to extremes; one should not assume that every process must be situation specific, just that some may be.

Not only may processes be situation specific, but they may also be person specific. Given that individual differences occur, it seems not unlikely that some of the processes governing behaviour may also exhibit individual differences in their occurrence. A process may occur in one individual, but be absent in another; alternatively, the importance of a process as a determinant of behaviour may vary. This point was first made by Allport (1937) who argued that not only do individuals vary with respect to position along a trait dimension but also with respect to the relevance of trait dimensions to explaining behaviour. In other words, individuals can differ in terms of the states of a hypothetical construct and they can also differ with respect to the importance a hypothetical construct (and the process in which the hypothetical construct occurs) has to the causation of behaviour. This is not to say that *all* psychological processes are subject to individual variation; however, individual variation, like inter-situation variation, must be considered as a possibility when extrapolating from data to theories. What may be a correct theory for one person may not be a correct theory for another.

The possibility that individuals may react differently to different treatments is seldom tested for, as analysis of experiments is usually limited to a comparison of group scores. Suppose, for example, that examination performance is measured in a non-drug and drug condition and that a significant improvement is found in the drug condition. The significant difference could result either because everyone's examination performance improves with the drug, or because only some people, for instance people high in test anxiety, show an improvement in exam performance. Although a comparison of group means would show an overall improvement in the drug condition, it cannot necessarily be inferred that the drug invariably improves examination performance, as the improvement may be limited to a fraction or even a very small minority of the sample. Hyland and Foot (1974) suggest that the best way to see if a treatment is producing a general effect over all the sample or a specific effect over just part of the sample is to consider the distribution of scores in different conditions. If there is an increased spread in a treatment condition, then one can conclude that individuals are reacting differentially to the treatment.

Psychological theories do appear, when compared with theories in other disciplines, to be rather difficult to test. The relationship between data and different possible theories is by no means always straightforward. Processes may be situation or person specific. Processes are difficult to isolate: when observing data to test one process one can never be sure that what is happening isn't caused by some other unspecified process. It is difficult to sort out what is happening when different processes contribute to the same be-haviour. These different problems have the consequence that it is often difficult to find unfavourable evidence for theories simply because unfavourable evidence may, with a little theoretical juggling, be attributed to something else. It is often difficult to falsify a psychological theory with one single piece of evidence and when this happens, the truth of a theory must be evaluated in terms of a number of slightly favourable or slightly unfavourable pieces of evidence, which together give some degree of confidence in the truth or falsity of the theory. Confirmation of psychological theories entails more uncertainty than confirmation of theories in other disciplines, but this problem must not be over-exaggerated. If there seems to be too much slightly unfavourable evidence, then it would seem reasonable to reject a theory; and it is because there is this possibility of rejection that psychological theories are scientific.

CONCLUDING REMARKS

Science does not proceed by separate acts of theory construction and theory testing, by a simple Popperian alternation of 'conjecture' and 'refutation'. Instead, theories are constructed and changed in the light of incoming data, in the light of incoming information about causal relations in the world. Although theory construction and theory testing have been examined under separate headings, the two should always proceed together. Theories must never be divorced from data nor should data be collected at random without theoretical guidance. The aim of theoretical psychology is to construct theories with high empirical content, theories which are capable of making powerful predictions. But a theory which is capable of making powerful predictions is no good to anyone if it is not true. Powerful predictions have little value if they do not occur.

It has been said by Popper, Bronowski and many others that a genuine modern science is characterised by tolerance. A true science must admit that its knowledge is based on uncertainty and that the explanations it provides may be incorrect. This book will, therefore conclude with a plea that psychologists should always act like true scientists. Theories are never proved to be true, but many people will believe that a theory, perhaps their own theory, is correct. This belief in the truth of a theory constitutes a necessary motivation for empirical studies and is part of the process of scientific enquiry. However, belief in the truth of a theory must always be governed by observation; it must not be governed by emotion. One should never try to 'prove' a theory with such fervour that all other theories and perhaps even unfavourable evidence is neglected. It is a characteristic of true scientific enquiry to be tolerant of the possibility that other alternative explanations may be shown eventually to be correct.

References

Allport, G. W., *Personality: a Psychological Interpretation.* Holt, Rinehart, Winston, 1937

Bem, D. J., and Allen, A., On predicting some of the people some of the time: the search for cross-situational consistency in behaviour. *Psychological Review*, 1974, **81**, 506–520

Blalock, H. M., *Causal Inferences in Non-experimental Research.* University of North Carolina Press, 1967

Blalock, H. M., Theory building and causal inferences. In H. M. Blalock and A. B. Blalock (Eds.), *Methodology in Social Research.* McGraw Hill, 1968

Borger, R., and Cioffi, F., *Explanation in the Behavioural Sciences.* Cambridge University Press, 1970

Bowers, K. S., Situationism in psychology. *Psychological Review*, 1973, **80**, 307–336

Broadbent, D. E., *Perception and Communication.* Pergamon Press, 1958

Brodbeck, M., Models, meaning and theories. In M. Brodbeck (Ed.), *Readings in the Philosophy of the Social Sciences.* Macmillan, 1968

Campbell, N. R., Definition of a theory. In R. Grandy (Ed.), *Theory and Observation in Science.* Prentice-Hall, 1973

Carnap, R., Logical foundations of the unity of science. In R. Carnap and C. W. Morris (Eds.), *International Encyclopedia of Unified Science*, Vol. 1, No. 1. University of Chicago Press, 1938

Cattell, R. B., *The Scientific Analysis of Personality.* Penguin, 1965

Chaplin, J. P., and Krawiec, T. S., *Systems and Theories of Psychology.* Holt, Rinehart, Winston, 1970

Coombs, C. H., Dawes, R. M., and Tversky, A., *Mathematical Psychology: an Elementary Introduction.* Prentice-Hall, 1970

Craik, K. J. W., *The Nature of Explanation.* Cambridge University Press, 1943 (reprinted 1967)

Cronbach, L. J., and Meehl, P. E., Construct validity in psychological tests. *Psychological Bulletin*, 1955, **52**, 281–302

Davidson, D., Actions, reasons, and causes. *Journal of Philosophy*, 1963, **60**, 685–700

Deutsch, J. A., *The Structural Basis of Behavior*. University of Chicago Press, 1960

Ekehammar, B., Interactionism in personality from a historical perspective. *Psychological Bulletin*, 1974, **81**, 1026–1048

Endler, N. S., and Magnusson, D., Toward an interactional psychology of personality. *Psychological Bulletin*, 1976, **83**, 956–974

Fodor, J. A., *Psychological Explanation*. Random House, 1968

Geach, P., and Black, M., *Philosophical Writings of Gottlob Frege*. Basil Blackwell, 1970

Gendron, B., On the relation of neurological and psychological theories: a critique of the hardware thesis. In R. C. Buck and R. S. Cohen (Eds.), *Boston Studies in the Philosophy of Science*. Reidel, 1971

Hanson, N. R., *Patterns of Discovery: an Inquiry into the Conceptual Foundations of Science*. Cambridge University Press, 1958

Harman, H. H., *Modern Factor Analysis*. Chicago University Press, 1967

Harré, R., and Secord, P. F., *The Explanation of Social Behaviour*. Basil Blackwell, 1972

Hedman, C. G., On when there must be a time difference between cause and effect. *Philosophy of Science*, 1972, **389**, 507–511

Heider, F., *The Psychology of Interpersonal Relations*. Wiley, 1958

Hempel, C. G., The theoretician's dilemma. A study in the logic of theory construction. In H. Feigl, M. Scriven, and G. Maxwell (Eds.), *Minnesota Studies in the Philosophy of Science*, Vol. 2. University of Minnesota Press, 1958

Hyland, M., and Foot, H., Group data, individual behaviour: a methodological note. *British Journal of Social and Clinical Psychology*, 1974, **13**, 93–95

Jeffrey, R. C., Remarks on explanatory power. In R. C. Buck and R. S. Cohen (Eds.), *Boston Studies in the Philosophy of Science*, Vol. 8. Reidel, 1971

Kantor, J. R., *The Scientific Evolution of Psychology*, Vol. 2. Principia Press, 1969

Kelly, G., *The Psychology of Personal Constructs*. Norton, 1955

Koffka, K., *Principles of Gestalt Psychology*. Harcourt Brace, 1935

Köhler, W., *Gestalt Psychology*. Liveright, 1947

Kuhn, T. S., *The Structure of Scientific Revolutions*. University of Chicago Press, 1962

Lakatos, L., History of science and its rational reconstruction. In R. C. Buck and R. S. Cohen (Eds.), *Boston Studies in the Philosophy of Science*, Vol. 8. Reidel, 1971

Lerner, M. J., and Matthews, G., Reactions to suffering of others under conditions of indirect responsibility. *Journal of Personality and Social Psychology*, 1967, **5**, 319–325

Lerner, M. J., and Simmons, C. H., Observer's reactions to the 'innocent victim': compassion or rejection? *Journal of Personality and Social Psychology*, 1966, **4**, 203–210

Lewin, K., *Principles of Topological Psychology*. McGraw-Hill, 1936

Lewin, K., The conceptual representation and the measurement of psychological forces. In D. K. Adams and H. Lundholm (Eds.), *Contributions to Psychological Theory*, Vol. 1. Duke University Press, 1938

Lewin, K., Defining the 'field at a given time'. *Psychological Review*, 1943, **50**, 292–310

McClelland, D. C., Atkinson, J. W., Clark, R. A., and Lowell, E. L., *The Achievement Motive*. Appleton-Century-Crofts, 1953

McDougall, W., *An Introduction to Social Psychology*. Methuen, 1908

Mack, R. W. and Snyder, R. C., The analysis of social conflict – toward an overview and synthesis. *Journal of Conflict Resolution*, 1957, **1**, 212–248

MacCorquodale, K., and Meehl, P. E., On a distinction between hypothetical constructs and intervening variables. *Psychological Review*, 1948, **55**, 95–107

Marx, M. H., and Goodson, F. E., *Theories in Contemporary Psychology*. Macmillan, 1976

Marx, M. H., and Hillix, W. A., *Systems and Theories in Psychology*. McGraw-Hill, 1973

Maxwell, G., The ontological status of theoretical entities. In H. Feigl and G. Maxwell (Eds.), *Minnesota Studies in the Philosophy of Science*, Vol. 3. University of Minnesota Press, 1962

Meehl, P. E., Psychological determinism and human rationality: A psychologist's reactions to Professor Karl Popper's 'of clouds and clocks'. In M. Radner and S. Winokur (Eds.), *Minnesota Studies in the Philosophy of Science*, Vol. 4. University of Minnesota Press, 1970

Michotte, A., *La perception de la causalité* Universitaires de Louvain, 1954

Miller, G. A., Galanter, E. H., and Pribram, K. H., *Plans and the Structure of Behavior*. Holt, Rinehart, Winston, 1960

Mischel, T., *Human Action: Conceptual and Empirical Issues*. Academic Press, 1969

Mischell, W., Toward a cognitive social learning reconceptualisation of personality. *Psychological Review*, 1973, **80**, 252–283

Murray, H. A., *Explorations in Personality*. Oxford University Press, 1938

Neel, A., *Theories of Psychology*. University of London Press, 1971

Osgood, C. E., Suci, G. J., and Tannenbaum, P. H., *The Measurement of Meaning*. University of Illinois Press, 1957

Peters, R. S., *The Concept of Motivation*. Routledge and Kegan Paul, 1958

Popper, K. R., *Conjectures and Refutations*. Routledge and Kegan Paul, 1963

Popper, K. R., *The Logic of Scientific Discovery*. Hutchinson, 1968 (revised edition)

Ramsay, F. P., *The Foundations of Mathematics*. Routledge and Kegan Paul, 1931

Reichenbach, H., *Experience and Prediction*. University of Chicago Press, 1938

Rosenthal, R., and Rosnow, R. L., *Artifact in Behavioural Research*. Academic Press, 1969

Rubin, Z., and Peplau, A., Belief in a Just World and reactions to another's lot: a study of participants in the national draft lottery. *Journal of Social Issues*, 1973, **29**, 73–93

Schultz, D. P., *The Science of Psychology: Critical Reflections*. Appleton-Century-Crofts, 1970

Sells, S. B., Dimensions of stimulus situations which account for behaviour variance. In S. B. Sells (Ed.), *Stimulus Determinants of Behaviour*. Ronald Press, 1963

Shallice, T., Dual functions of consciousness. *Psychological Review*, 1972, **79**, 383–393

Shaw, M. E., and Costanzo, P. R., *Theories of Social Psychology*. McGraw-Hill, 1970

Sherif, M., and Sherif, C. W., *Social Psychology*. Harper and Row, 1969

Skinner, B. F., *Beyond Freedom and Dignity*. Jonathan Cape, 1972

Skinner, B. F., Behaviourism at fifty. *Science*, 1963, **90**, 951–958

Sternberg, S., The discovery of processing stages: extension of Donder's method. *Acta Psychologica*, 1969, **30**, 276–315

Tizard, J., Psychology and social policy. Presidential address to the British Psychological Society. *Bulletin of the British Psychological Society*, 1976, **29**, 225–234

Tuomela, R., *Theoretical Concepts*. Springer-Verlag, 1973

Underwood, B. J., Individual differences as a crucible in theory construction. *American Psychologist*, 1975, **30**, 128–134

Wann, T. W., *Behaviorism and Phenomenology*. University of Chicago Press, 1964

Whittaker, J. O., Resolution of the communication discrepancy issue in attitude change. In C. Sheriff and M. Sheriff (Eds.), *Attitudes, Ego-involvement and Change*. Wiley, 1968

Williams, R. M., *The Reduction of Intergroup Tensions*. Social Science Research Council, 1947

Wolman, B. B., *Contemporary Theories and Systems in Psychology*. Harper and Row, 1960

Woodworth, R. S., *Experimental Psychology*. Wiley, 1938

Zeeman, E. C., *Catastrophe Theory: Selected Papers*. Addison Wesley, 1977

Zuckerman, M., Belief in a just world and altruistic behaviour. *Journal of Personality and Social Psychology*, 1975, **31**, 972–976

Further Reading

CHAPTER 1

Advantages and disadvantages of theories

Hempel, C. G., The theoretician's dilemma. A study in the logic of theory construction. In H. Feigl, M. Scriven and G. Maxwell (Eds.), *Minnesota Studies in the Philosophy of Science*, Vol. 2. University of Minnesota Press, 1958

Maxwell, G., The ontological status of theoretical entities. In H. Feigl and G. Maxwell (Eds.), *Minnesota Studies in the Philosophy of Science*, Vol. 3. University of Minnesota Press, 1962

Skinner, B. F., *Beyond Freedom and Dignity*. Jonathan Cape, 1972

Wann, T. W., *Behaviorism and Phenomenology*. University of Chicago Press, 1964

History of Science

Kuhn, T. S., *The Structure of Scientific Revolutions*. University of Chicago Press, 1962

Lakatos, L., History of science and its rational reconstruction. In R. C. Buck and R. S. Cohen (Eds.), *Boston Studies in the Philosophy of Science*, Vol. 8. Reidel, 1971

CHAPTER 2

Explanatory Power

Popper, K. R., *The Logic of Scientific Discovery*. Hutchinson. Revised edition, 1968

Jeffrey, R. C., Remarks on explanatory power. In R. C. Buck and

R. S. Cohen (Eds.), *Boston Studies in the Philosophy of Science*, Vol. 8. Reidel, 1971

Form and Content

Brodbeck, M., Models, meaning and theories. In M. Brodbeck (Ed.), *Readings in the Philosophy of Science*. Macmillan, 1968
Campbell, N. R., Definition of a theory. In R. Grandy (Ed.), *Theory and Observation in Science*. Prentice-Hall, 1973

Mathematical Models

Coombs, C. H., Dawes, R. M., and Tversky, A., *Mathematical Psychology: An Elementary Introduction*. Prentice-Hall, 1970
Zeeman, E. C., *Catastrophe Theory: Selected Papers*. Addison Wesley, 1977

Observable/Theoretical Distinction

Hanson, N. R., *Patterns of discovery: An Inquiry into the Conceptual Foundations of Science*. Cambridge University Press, 1958
Maxwell, G., The ontological status of theoretical entities. In H. Feigl and G. Maxwell (Eds.), *Minnesota Studies in the Philosophy of Science*, Vol. 3. University of Minnesota Press, 1962

CHAPTER 3

MacCorquodale, K. and Meehl, P. E., On a distinction between hypothetical constructs and intervening variables. *Psychological Review*, 1948, **55**, 95–107
Cronbach, K. and Meehl, P. E., Construct validity in psychological tests. *Psychological Bulletin*, 1955, **52**, 281–302

CHAPTER 9

Rosenthal, R., and Rosnow, R. L., *Artifact in Behavioral Research*. Academic Press, 1969

Schultz, D. P., *The Science of Psychology: Critical Reflections.* Appleton-Century-Crofts, 1970

GENERAL

Borger, R., and Cioffi, F., *Explanation in the Behavioural Sciences.* Cambridge University Press, 1970

Chaplin, J. P., and Krawiec, T. S., *Systems and Theories of Psychology.* Holt, 1970

Marx, M. H., and Goodson, F. E., *Theories in Contemporary Psychology.* Macmillan, 1976

Marx, M. H., and Hillix, W. A., *Systems and Theories in Psychology.* McGraw-Hill, 1973

Mischel, T., *Human Action: Conceptual and Empirical Issues.* Academic Press, 1969

Shaw, M. E., and Costanzo, P. R., *Theories of Social Psychology.* McGraw-Hill, 1970

Wolman, B. B., *Contemporary Theories and Systems in Psychology.* Harper and Row, 1960